D1445619

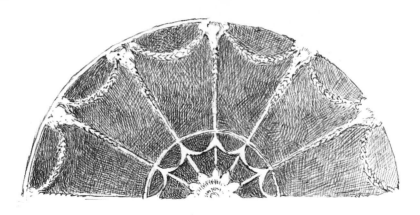

FANLIGHTS

FANLIGHTS

Alexander Stuart Gray
John Sambrook

Drawings by Charlotte Halliday

The American Institute of Architects Press
Washington, D.C.

© in the texts by Stuart Gray, John Sambrook,
Tony Birks-Hay
© in the drawings and watercolours
Charlotte Halliday

Published by the American Institute of
Architects Press, Washington, D.C. 20006.
First published in UK in 1990 by
A & C Black (Publishers) Ltd
35 Bedford Row, London WC1R 4JH
Designed by Alphabet & Image Ltd
Sherborne, Dorset, UK.
93 92 91 90 7 6 5 4 3 2 1

Library of Congress Cataloging-in-Publication Data
Gray, Alexander Stuart.
   Fanlights: a visual architectural history/text by Alexander Stuart
Gray, John Sambrook; drawings by Charlotte Halliday.
      p.   cm.
   Includes bibliographical references.
   ISBN 1-55835-062-4: $21.95
   1. Fanlights—Great Britain.   2. Architecture, Georgian—Great
Britain.   3. Architecture Domestic—Great Britain.   4. Fanlights—
United States.   5. Architecture, Georgian—United States.
6. Architecture, Domestic—United States.   I. Sambrook, John.
II. Halliday, Charlotte.   III. Title.
NA3030.G73   1990
728—dc20   89-48840
                            CIP

On the half title page is a drawing of a
fanlight in the High Street, Arundel, Sussex.
The title page shows No. 43 South Hill Park,
Bury St Edmunds, Suffolk, an early timber
fanlight. On the facing page is the fanlight at
No. 30 Claremont Square, Islington.

Printed in Great Britain by BAS Printers
Limited, Stockbridge, Hampshire

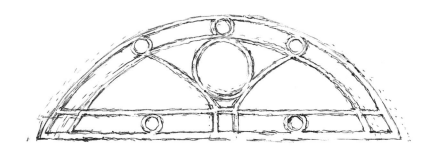

Contents

Introduction 6
Tony Birks-Hay

Inspiration and realisation 10

Construction and repair 19
John Sambrook

Glossary 30

London 32

Country towns 80

Bath 93

Bristol 100

Edinburgh New Town 113

Dublin 121

Fanlights of Colonial and Federal America 131
Tony Birks-Hay

Bibliography 144

Acknowledgements 146

Index 147

9 Queen Anne's Gate, London, headquarters of the Architectural Press, has inner and outer fanlights fashioned by using ogee curved wood glazing bars as in some window heads of the period. Identical designs can be found across the Atlantic.

Introduction

Strange it is that the fanlight, ornate jewel of the Georgian town house, should have been overlooked until now by architectural historians as a subject in its own right. English publishing houses still tend to cluster in Bloomsbury around the British Museum and in other once-genteel residential areas of the great city of London. As with solicitors and architects, the size of their operations is often appropriate to space once residential in purpose, and it is not surprising therefore that a host of publishers located in Georgian terraces have fanlights over their front entrances. Not all of them pass in and out without recognising the architectural individuality over their heads, and indeed at least two publishers have chosen a fanlight as their company's particular symbol. Others use the fanlighted doorway of their premises as an eloquent invitation on their catalogues. It implies both prestige and enlightenment.

Histories of the architecture of the appropriate period illustrate Georgian door-ways with their delicious overdoor windows, without referring to the fanlights themselves. Anonymous, they remain unmentioned in the index, and their history, unlike that of other architectural details and furniture, remains unrecorded.

There is a danger in examining the different fanlights in isolation from their original context, a danger which I hope that this present and pioneering book avoids. But examined in isolation they must be, if any sensible and comparative study is ever to be published, for if one takes into account the door case, the door, footscraper and the railings, one is bound to consider Georgian architecture as a mirror of Georgian life, ground well covered not only for London but for numerous English, Scottish, Irish and indeed American towns.

Attention to detail and a generally high level of craftsmanship was taken for granted in the eighteenth, nineteenth and early twentieth century, much of it to disappear with the ravages of the two world wars. It has been replaced by mass-produced units to fill the openings of, or even to clad the skeletal structures of, the buildings of the present age.

On a domestic scale the manufacture of prefabricated windows and doors now seems to be left in the hands of those with no architectural or aesthetic training, no schooling in the rules of proportion which caused Robert Adam, hero of this present book, to make openings a focus and a source of wonder. Against a background of metrication and standard brick sizes, modular windows are chur-ned out with proportions only matched in their mindless ugliness by the lack of sensitivity over the cutting of mouldings and the weight of glazing bars.

The astonishing success in the 1980s of the so-called 'Regency door', the light-weight hardwood mutation with a fan-shaped opening slightly above chest height, has no little significance in the appearance of our book. For the many thousands who laugh at this absurd little door, and reflect on the Georgian doorway which had an influence on its clumsy realisation, how many, I wonder, are aware of the hundreds and indeed thousands of original and unique fanlight designs which still exist over the doors of ordinary houses in every city and town in Great Britain?

It is not the continued existence, in spite of bombing and 150 years of neglect, of fanlights in such numbers, but the variety in design and execution of these windows which this book is about. Both author and illustrator from their different points of view have related fanlight design to their personal interest in music. Just as the octave with the effects of rhythm, of intervals and repetitions, has an infinite poten-tial for variation, so the sliced-orange hemicycle of the classic fanlight or the rectangle which succeeded it gives the architect, joiner, designer and metal foundry the opportunity for an infinity of designs. The two hundred or so illustrations in this book give only a hint of the variety which can be found. Since nearly all towns and villages in the British Isles have roots more than 200 years old, it is reasonable that fanlights should appear in every one of these towns, and in a great many villages as well.

Inevitably the geographical spectrum of the present work is more limited, begin-ning with London, home of both author and illustrator, but the city-by-city arrangement, I believe, succeeds in its aim of reflecting the local character of fanlights, from the neo-Gothic of Cheltenham and the self-confident authority of Edinburgh, to the two areas where fanlights flower and overflow into their most spectacular form.

The first of these is Dublin, where invention and exuberance in the eighteenth century contrast with recent neglect. The second area is on the opposite side of the Atlantic. All across the eastern states of North America fanlights are to be found, and in fact are much more appreciated than in Britain. For scintillating elaboration and in decorative exuberance none approaches those of Salem and Boston, Massachusetts.

The Georgian era, and the early Federal period in New England, were times of invention, not copying. As conservation is now in full swing, American restorers must take credit for the faithfulness of their work, while the proponents of neo-Georgian architecture in Britain must take the blame for taking only cursory glances at detailing and the techniques of their architectural forebears, as in the fanlights over six restored houses in Broadwick Street, Soho, London, where standard metal window sections have the flat side facing the street. It is hoped that John Sambrook's chapter on restoration, in which he generously explains his hard-won techniques for reconstruction, will help to correct this and will make this book a useful and practical guide to the architectural future as well as an illuminating glimpse into our architectural past.

Wherever stone and wood are used for building, especially in high latitudes, the fanlight in some form is to be found. Its architectural study depends on the starting point. As indicated in the Introduction, English-influenced Georgian architecture with fanlights is found in all areas of British expansion in the eighteenth and nineteenth centuries. The most venerable houses in Australia have fanlights, as in South Africa, Bermuda, Barbados, even St Helena, and the Federal Americans created their own magnificent hybrids.

If, however, in Northern Europe one takes as a starting point another country, a different perspective emerges. In France, from Alençon to Lille and down to Angoulême and Lyon, tall haughty fanlights owing nothing to Adam but a great deal to decorative European ironwork tradition, are dominant, and a fine collection is gathered in *Architecture de France a travers les Croquis d'Albert Laprade* (Ecole des Beaux Arts 1903). In Belgium, where sometimes murky light calls for as much window as possible, fanlights are again tall, symmetrical, but often not contained by a semicircle or rectangle. A segmental arch is common, and sometimes the door lintel at the window's base will itself be curved, as seen in such towns as Namur and Auvelais, as indeed in Spain and Portugal.

The high ground-floor rooms in the old towns of the Low Countries mean fanlights taller yet again, sometimes taller than they are wide, with patterns ornate like peacocks' tails or the lyre shaped tails of Birds of Paradise. Iron grilles in front of single sheets of overdoor glass are more common in Continental Europe than in Britain, and their traditional use continued throughout the nineteenth century, so that patterned overdoor windows are still in use in the Art Nouveau houses of Brussels, long after the fanlight had fallen from favour in England.

Once the architectural amateur has been caught by the subject, fanlights strike the eye. A collector of, say, Georgian silver can go on extending his field of interest and can trace design influences from many quarters, but he will, if he is to contain his subject, specialize. So Charlotte Halliday has specialized, in illustrating this book; but the search does not stop here: it has merely begun.

Tony Birks-Hay

This beautiful doorway in teak in the rococo style from the Normal School, Cape Town, South Africa, has been ascribed to the sculptor Andreas Andrydt. The measured drawings by P. W. Robertson indicate that the fanlight was glazed with individual panes — it is not a grille.

A tiny teardrop fanlight in Maunsel Street, Pimlico, London SW1.

Inspiration and realisation

Between 1725 and 1825, the cities and towns of Britain and Ireland created in their new terraces, squares, crescents and circuses, settings for that jewel in their façades, the overdoor or fanlight.

London, Edinburgh, Dublin, Bristol and Bath developed each in its own way—London and Dublin in brick, Edinburgh and Bath in stone, Bristol in brick and stone. Inspiration for the new brick style came from London, where the disastrous fire of 1666 had led to a total change in the materials and method of construction. On the advice of the Surveyor-General (Sir) Christopher Wren, in place of the lath-and-plastered wood framing of the houses, their steep gables, their overhanging storeys and bow windows, a new city arose, a city of solid brick walls crowned by brick parapets, their roofs running parallel to the street.

Lacking the variety of the Elizabethan and Jacobean streets what, then, were these new streets, so sober and so practical, to look like? The Royal Architect, Inigo Jones, had already introduced at Westminster, St James's and Greenwich, the Italian style of well-proportioned windows widely spaced in plain walls. And soon the Dutch were to invent windows with wood sashes made to slide up and down. In 1688, by a quirk of events, Wren found he was to serve Dutch King William, who had come over to share the throne of England with his wife, Queen Mary, and so the great additions Wren made to their palaces at Kensington and Hampton Court suited the Dutch taste.

But in approaching our theme, we run ahead too fast. We must first turn backwards to events and the individuals who took part in them; first inspiration, then information, and finally realisation.

To satisfy a thirst for knowledge of Ancient Rome, and anxious that the family's palaces and churches should reflect in some measure its glories, Lorenzo di Medici in 1404 sent two young men to Rome. They were to measure and report upon those buildings still above ground which had survived the sackings, the burnings and the pillaging of a thousand years. The movement to be called 'Il Rinascimento', or 'La Renaissance', was now under way. The two young men sent upon this voyage of discovery were Filippo Brunelleschi, aged twenty-six, an architect, and Donato di Nicolo di Betto Bardi, called Donatello, not yet seventeen, a sculptor. Both were

10

guildsmen of the illustrious 'Guild of the Goldsmiths' of Florence. This meant that they were recognised already as craftsmen of a high order, for the Guild included not only workers in precious metals, but painters, sculptors, engineers and archi-tects. Brunelleschi was to become Florence's greatest architect, Donatello her finest sculptor. Confronted by the great size of the columns and cornices still in use, or half-buried or lying about in confusion, the young men were fortunate, for the high quality and great delicacy of the arts of Florence where they had been trained prepared them to regard with caution the grandeur of Rome. Fortunate, too, are we, who can enjoy today the graceful white vaults, the serene arches of grey silk-smooth pietra-serena in the churches of San Lorenzo and Santo Spirito, in the Chapel of the Pazzi and in the arcades of the foundling hospital, presided over by the supreme dome of S. Maria del Fiore. Fortunate are we also for Donatello's 'The Young David' and 'Saint George', and for the tragic figure of the ageing 'S. Maria Magdalene'.

Three and a half centuries later another young man, also twenty-six years of age, left his native city to pay his first visit to Rome. The year was 1754, the young man was Robert Adam, second of the four sons of William Adam, a successful architect of Edinburgh, the city called later 'Athens of the North'. The Rome which greeted Adam in 1754 had changed much since 1404. Some of the ancient buildings had sunk further into decay, some were buried even deeper under the debris of another three centuries. Some, fortunate enough to continue in use, appeared just as the two Florentines had found them. The Popes had returned long since from their 'Babylonian Captivity' at Avignon. The patrician families of Rome, joined by successful bankers from Florence, the Medici and the Chigi, had built great palaces and villas there. St Peter's basilica had been rebuilt by six architects in succession, and treatises on the new Roman style had been published by Alberti, Scamozzi, Serlio, Palladio and Vignola.

Making the best of his visit to Rome, Robert Adam was made a member of the exclusive Academy of St Luke and met the great draughtsman Giovanni Battista Piranesi. Three years later, accompanied by the French architect Charles Louis Clerisseau, Robert Adam visited Venice. Their purpose was not to study there, but to obtain from the Doge permission to make a long visit to Spalato in Dalmatia (now Yugoslavia). Here the Roman Emperor Diocletian had built a great palace for his retirement, for he was born in Dalmatia at Dioclete. So vast were the remains of this palace by the sea that the town (now called Split) had grown up within it, the walls of the palace becoming the fortifications of the town.

It was not surprising that the Venetian governor, suspecting Robert Adam and his party of being spies, yet obliged to comply with the Doge's orders, limited their stay to five weeks. Undeterred, the resourceful Scot had brought with him two draughtsmen. As Adam reported later, 'By dint of unwearied application' the party returned with enough information for Adam to publish in 1763 the great folio volume of sixty-one plates and thirty-one pages under the title *Ruins of the Palace of the Emperor Diocletian at Spalarto in Dalmatia* (Robert Adam retained the 'r' in Spalarto) by R. Adam FRS, FSA, architect to the King and to the Queen, printed for the author MDCCLXIIII. Among the subscribers were Ralph Allen Esq. (the 'Man of Bath'), Lord Mansfield of Kenwood House, James Stuart Esq. (*Antiquities of Athens*), the Doge of Venice, Gio. Batt. Piranesi, Architetto Veneto, Il Sign. Antonio Zucchi pittore da Venezia, M. Charles Louis Clerisseau.

In his preface Robert Adam affirmed, 'Assiduity and repeated observations enabled me to surmount difficulties.' And among those difficulties would have been surveying on the Adriatic coast in July in the broadcloth and heavy tricorn hats of the period, as depicted in his drawings.

In the dedication of his work to George III, Robert Adam wrote:

> *At this happy Period, when Great Britain enjoys the Peace, the Reputation and Power she has acquired by Arms, your Majesty's Singular attention to the Art of Elegance promises an Age of Perfection that will compleate the Glories of your Reign and fix an Era no less remarkable than that of Pericles, Augustus and the Medicis.*

At Spalato Robert Adam found support for the ideas already in his mind for the rejuvenation of contemporary architecture as practised in Britain by William Kent under the aegis of Lord Burlington and by Sir William Chambers. In those days of Palladian conformity, a significant change discovered by Adam at Spalato was a new form of column capital—a simple band of palm leaves encircling it—differing from the orthodox Ionic, Corinthian and Composite which had been used by the mainland Romans and, a thousand years later, by the Italians, French and British in turn. This capital Robert Adam illustrated in Plate XLIX of his great work on Spalato, and titled 'Capital and Pilaster in the Angle of the Peristylium of the Temple of Aesculapius'.

A discovery at Spalato of even more significance for Adam was an opening in the Peristylium of the Palace, a centre arch with lintelled sidelights—a style of opening called to this day a Palladian window, because it was used by Andrea Palladio at the Basilica at Vicenza to overcome the difficulty of spanning the width between piers of an earlier building (although Sebastiano Serlio had published this idea ten years earlier).

At Spalato Adam found evidence also of the influence the arts of Greece continued to exert upon ornamental carving in the eastern parts of the Roman Empire, an influence to be found in the ruins at Baalbec and Palmyra. In the first volume of the *Antiquities of Athens*, published by James Stuart and Nicholas Revett in 1762, appeared drawings of the works of the 'Periclean Age', the fifth century BC, enough to provide Adam with authentic details for his favourite anthemion (honeysuckle), palmette, and other decorative motifs for his 'new style', a style soon to be known as the 'Adam Style'.

The inspiration Adam derived from Spalato was not confined to capitals or to the decoration of pilasters. The ruins had provided him with evidence of the shallow segmental curved vault and arch appropriate to the courts of a palace and preferable to the great vaults Adam had seen at the Roman Baths at the Basilica of Constantine, and in the dome of the Pantheon. This shallower and lighter vault was continued with even greater effect by Sir John Soane at the Bank of England (wilfully demolished in 1930), and in other works of his.

Later, in his preface to the first volume of *Works in Architecture of Robert and James Adam*, published in 1773, Robert Adam wrote:

To enter upon an enquiry into the state of this art in Great Britain, till the late changes it has undergone is no part of our present designs. We leave that subject to the observation of the skilful who, we doubt not, will easily perceive within these few years a remarkable improvement in the form, convenience, arrangement and variety in the outside composition and in the decoration of the inside an almost total change. (Vol.1, page 3)

The massive entablature, the ponderous compartment ceiling, the tabernacle frame almost the only species of ornament formerly known in the country are now universally exploded and in their place we have adopted a beautiful variety of light mouldings, gracefully formed, delicately enriched and arranged with propriety and skill. We have introduced a great diversity of ceilings, friezes and decorated pilasters and have added grace and beauty to the whole by a mixture of grotesque stucco, and painted ornaments, together with the flowering rainceau with its fanciful figures and winding foliage. (Vol.1, page 4)

Thus did Robert Adam indicate that the skilled among the public would make their own decision regarding the improvements he was advocating with such subtlety. The skilful did indeed make their choice, and Robert Adam was appointed in 1761 'Architect of the King's Works'. He had already built his first public building, the Screen in Whitehall to hide Thomas Ripley's ill-proportioned Admiralty Building of 1723-6. As Sir William Chambers was appointed Architect of the King's Works alongside Robert Adam in 1761 it is not surprising to find Chambers resenting the presumption of Robert Adam's remarks, and not surprising either that Adam was never admitted to the new Royal Academy of Arts of which Chambers was the first Treasurer in 1768.

James Wyatt, although he was to adopt many of Adam's innovations, wrote to George II: 'There have been no new architecture since Sir William Chambers .... When I came from Italy I found the Public Taste corrupted by the Adams and was obliged to comply with it'—a double blow at Robert Adam. It was a century of intrigue, professional jealousy and spite.

A long view of the manners, fashions and personalities of the eighteenth century in Britain reveals similarities between the arts of architecture and music. A comparative view of music and architecture reveals that James Gibbs, architect of the Senate House, Cambridge, The Radcliffe Camera, Oxford, and an architect of the London churches of St Mary-le-Strand and of St Martin-in-the-Fields, was born three years before J.S. Bach and G.F. Handel, and that Sir William Chambers, architect for the rebuilding of Somerset House, London, was born, we find, in 1723, nine years before Joseph Haydn. This brings us to compare the birth dates of Robert Adam with that of Wolfgang Amadeus Mozart. Each, by his own art, exerted a strong influence upon the art and fashion of the last quarter of their century. We find Adam completing his first public building in 1760 when Mozart's first compositions were being published. Adam provided the appropriate setting for the minuet and for the chamber music of Mozart and his contemporaries.

For their successes Robert and James Adam did not depend entirely upon the plans and fabric of their town houses and country mansions, upon their reno-vations, re-modelling and extensions. The Adam Style depended equally upon the design of their ceilings, mirrors and over-mantels, their statuary, marble fireplaces and their designs for door furniture which they issued to special manufacturers. Carpets and furniture, too, had to conform. It was not enough to rely upon the designs for furniture of Hepplewhite or Sheridan, elegant and tasteful though they were. The Adams' achievement was a unification of all detailing in their revolu-tionary style. This, at last, brings us to our subject, the overdoor window most properly called fanlight in deference to the Adam influence.

In the new streets, squares and crescents being built around London, Bath, Clifton, Dublin and Edinburgh, as the Adam influence grew, the terrace house was the principal component. The frontage of the terrace house was restricted most often to two windows and an entrance door. The unity of the whole street or square depended upon the repetition of identical frontages, crowned by a cornice of identical design or by a plain parapet. The one distinguishing mark where varia-tion was expected and welcome was the surround to the entrance door, the door-case. This could be embellished by a surround of stone, wood or plaster, according to the locality, and any of the three 'Orders' of column or pilaster could be used, and the 'entablature' they carried could be raised into a 'pediment', triangular, curved or 'broken'. Prominent in the town houses of the brothers was the fanlight over the entrance door to admit light to the entrance lobby. With radiating spokes from a central orb, round-topped overdoor windows of this earlier type (see page 18) became delicate, intricate, traceried fans to match in their elegance the identically named accessories of Georgian ladies.

Charlotte Halliday's drawings in this book show how quickly elegance and diversity in fanlights spread, especially in the estates to the north of central London.

In the typical town house the entrance door led to a lobby, sometimes to an inner door, which could have its own fanlight, and finally to the staircase, an arrange-ment called sometimes the 'Dutch plan'. These entrance doorways, whether in Truro, Dublin or Aberdeen, whether of stone, wood or plaster, show no regional differences; they are correct down to the tiniest moulding. How did this happen? First of all we must look to the fashion for the 'Grand Tour', a fashion which demanded of the great landowners and country gentry that they send their sons, under the instruction of a tutor, often a clergyman, to visit the cities of Italy and to make acquaintance with the buildings illustrated in the great folios which every nobleman had in his library.

When most of the town houses and village houses were on land belonging to the nobility, to the Church or to a City Company, there was little need for the control of any other authority, should one have existed. No craftsman would dare to put up anything which the duke's agent or his architect would condemn, even if the noble

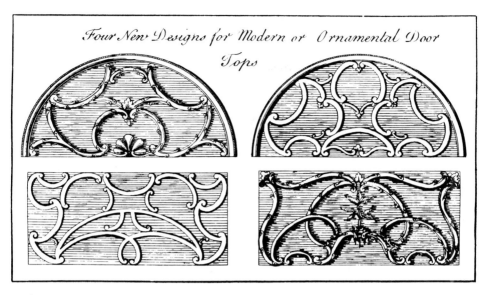

John Crunden in 1770 issued 'The Joiner and Cabinet Maker's Darling', illustrating designs for these 'Door Tops' as he called them. His designs, intended for wood, would have been carried out by craftsmen well versed in the making of chair-backs of the type introduced by Thomas Chippendale (1718–79). These four patterns for door tops in wood in the rococo style of the period are innocent of the new designs introduced by Robert Adam intended for construction in metal. Notice how Crunden's designs, in their fluidity, suit either rounded or rectangular openings. They would have been carried out in a fine-grained wood such as lime or cherry. Examples of this style can be seen on pages 79 and 85.

lord himself had not spotted it already from his coach, or the squire from his horse. And so, for the guidance of the owners of the estates, their agents and their architects, appeared the Books of Architecture and the Pattern Books.

The first guide book of this kind predated Adam, and was by the great architect James Gibbs, who produced *Rules for Drawing the Several Parts of Architecture* in 1732: 'a publication much employed by eighteenth-century master builders and [which] in this way had a great influence on architectural design both in England and in America' (H.M. Colvin, from *A Biographical Dictionary of English Architects, 1660-1840*). At the same time as Gibbs's books came Batty Langley's *Builders' Jewel, or the Youth's Instructor and Workman's Remembrancer*, and among a half-dozen of his similar books of instruction *Ancient Architecture Restored and Improved by Rules and Proportions*. John Crunden, an architect himself, published in 1768 *Convenient and Ornamental Architecture*, consisting of 'Original Designs for Plans, Elevations and Sections from the Farm House to the Most grand and magnificent Villa', and in 1770 *The Joiner and Cabinet Maker's Darling*, in which were 'Four Designs for Modern and Ornamental Door-tops' (see above).

At this date the currents of Adam's revolutionary designs and the more work-manlike examples of patterns based on carpentry forms ran together, producing a steady flow of ideas: Chippendale, neo-Classical, neo-gothic. In fanlights the batswing and the teardrop forms made their appearance, to be followed in turn by interlacing geometrical forms. The pattern books continued to flow forth.

From William Halfpenny, who worked as an architect in Bristol and elsewhere, came more than a dozen handbooks of designs, sometimes under the alias of 'Michael Hoare'. Early in the next century the architect Matthew Cottingham published *The Ornamental Metal Worker's Director*, and the next year an enlarged version titled *The Smith and Founder's Director*, containing a series of 'Designs and Patterns for Ornamental Iron and Brass Works'.

The manufacturers of fanlights and suchlike appurtenances for the building trade began to issue catalogues, and so we find in London Underwood, Bottomley and Hamble of High Holborn issuing catalogues from 1780 to 1831, and several dozen designs from Joseph Bottomley of Cheapside, a catalogue from Underwood and Doyle and one from The Eldorado Patent Sash Company of Gerrard Street, Soho. Other catalogues came from I. & J. Taylor of Holborn, and from McNamara of Church Row, Houndsditch.

Unless the designs specified it, the pattern books did not indicate any specific material for the various architectural details on which they gave guidance. The result was that a stone gate pier, for instance, can have panels which imitate wood panelling and the imitation of leatherwork would appear in stone or in wood.

Likewise, when fanlights had to be made from the designs shown in the pattern books, the craftsman had to employ much ingenuity to make them both windtight and rainproof. Earlier designs in wood sometimes assumed the character of a chair-back as made by Chippendale (see pages 80 and 84). When the designs were too delicate for wood, wrought iron, cast iron, lead and even brass castings and 'compo' had to be used to combine strength with delicacy, as John Sambrook explains in the succeeding chapter.

When the Adam Style dictated overdoor windows, the appropriate ornaments, festoons, loops and pendants could be made only by specialists working in centres such as London, and distributed to the far corners of the islands by road and canal, and by sea to the far corners of the British Empire. Before Independence, fanlights were shipped across to the American Colonies. In the Federal Period which followed, pattern books were published in America and distinctive fanlights were made in the Republic, as indicated on page 134.

RIGHT *At 14 and also at 13 Erskine Hill, Hampstead Garden Suburb, London NW11, a wooden fanlight, designed by the architect Edwin Lutyens in 1910, does not hold glass, for behind it a staircase climbs to the first floor. Lutyens, working here in the William and Mary style of Wren, enjoyed playing the same trick as did Wren in the Fountain Court of Hampton Court Palace, where the arches, reaching above the first floor, meet the problem with a similar disguise. Although composed of nine identical pieces of wood, Lutyens has arranged them to produce a richly varied rococo design. Here wit combines with elegance; Lutyens' mother was Irish.*

Construction and repair of fanlights

John Sambrook

Construction

It may seem a rather obvious statement, but a fanlight is only a window which has been treated prettily because of its position over the front door. For this reason early fanlights were made in the same way as ordinary windows, which meant that, by 1700, the double-hung sliding sash, which had superseded leaded casements in any building displaying the merest hint of architectural pretension. One of the factors in the development of the sash window was the availability of suitable glass, so one must begin by looking at the ways in which glass was made in the seventeenth and eighteenth centuries.

In Elizabethan times, when furnaces were wood-fired, glass making on a small scale was widely spread over Britain, wherever suitable sand and woodland were found together. However, in 1615 concern over the destruction of forests caused the King to issue both a Proclamation forbidding the burning of wood in glasshouses, and a Royal Patent which gave a monopoly of glass making by the coal-fired process to Sir Robert Mansell. After a number of false starts, Mansell established his enterprise in Newcastle-on-Tyne where coal was cheap and cases of glass could easily be shipped to London, packed amongst the coal, in the fleet of colliers serving the east coast ports. Although the monopoly was broken in 1640, Mansell rebuilt his furnaces after the Civil War and, despite competition from other glasshouses, Newcastle remained the principal source of window glass until the end of the eighteenth century.

The past fifty years have seen considerable advances in the methods of manu-facturing glass but, until 1930, most ordinary window glass was made by an improved version of the 'muff' process, which, in the eighteenth century, produced

LEFT *36 Bedford Row, London WC1. We are fortunate in finding an early wooden fanlight contemporary with the splendid doorway, both from the early eighteenth century. The spokes, resembling those of the coach wheels of the period, are joined at the top, not by an arch, but by a delicately carved pair of brackets, springing from a tiny capital at the head of each tapering spoke. The spandrels over the arch and the brackets supporting the cornice are equally well carved in the manner of Grinling Gibbons, Wren's carver. Compare with No. 25 Church Row, Hampstead, London NW3, on page 71.*

'broad' or 'common' glass, in contrast to glass made by the 'spun crown' method. In each case manufacture began with a glassblower gathering a considerable quantity of molten 'metal' onto his pipe and blowing it into a globe. Thereafter the processes diverged. In the case of muff glass the globe was greatly elongated, by repeatedly reheating and blowing, whilst swinging the pipe over a pit. When the ends were cut off, the result was a cylinder, perhaps 18 inches in diameter by 60 inches long. This cylinder was, whilst still hot, slit along its length with iron shears and opened out into a flat sheet by reheating it over a metal plate covered in sand. Although this method produced sheets of fairly large size, contact with the plate, and the wooden bats used to flatten it out, resulted in a finish of such indifferent quality, much subject to specks and blemishes, that broad glass was hardly used in buildings of quality during the Georgian period.

The best window glass was produced by the 'crown' method in which the glassblower's initial globe was first attached, by a nodule of molten glass, to a plain iron rod at a point directly opposite the entry of the blowpipe, which was then broken out. The incomplete globe, attached to the rod, was then ready for the most skilled part of the operation; the glassmaker returned it to the furnace and kept it spinning rapidly until, suddenly, when the glass had become sufficiently mobile, it would fly out, under centrifugal force, into a disc some four feet in diameter. The moment this occurred the disc was removed from the fire and kept spinning until it had hardened sufficiently to be cut free. The discs, or 'tables', were then removed to an annealing furnace, to be reheated and allowed to cool slowly, to remove internal stresses.

Although tables of crown glass involved much wastage in the cutting, by reason of their circular shape and the more-or-less useless central bullion where the iron had been attached, and were subject to slight concentric rings of optical distortion, their lustre and clarity could not be matched, and, throughout the eighteenth century, crown glass, whether from Newcastle or London, was universally specified for the better classes of work.

Whilst glassmakers in England were perfecting crown glass, continental manufacturers devoted themselves to improving the cylinder method and, in 1832, Lucas Chance introduced these continental improvements to his factory in Stourbridge. By slitting the cylinders, cold, with a diamond and opening them out over a bed of glass, rather than sand, it was possible to overcome the usual objections to broad glass, and the advantages of larger sheets, and the lack of waste, resulted in a rapid decline in crown glassmaking, despite its superior lustre. Some small tables of crown glass are still spun today, but solely for the decorative effect of the bullions, ironically the very parts that a Georgian glazier would have discarded, or sold off cheap to those who could afford no better.

From this brief review, it will be appreciated that, before the 1830s, pane sizes in the better sorts of glass were quite severely limited. With leaded casements this had not mattered, because the ability of the leads to withstand wind pressure limited pane sizes to about 6 by 4 inches, but the introduction of sash windows, with timber glazing bars, permitted a reappraisal of traditional glazing patterns. It was not long before confidence in the new windows permitted the glazing to fall into the familiar and satisfying pattern, now perceived as a hallmark of the Georgian period, in which each sash is divided by two vertical glazing bars and as many horizontals as will give openings roughly one-and-a-half times as high as they are wide; a formula that very commonly produces panes of $10\frac{1}{2}$ by 15 inches, which is about as large as can be cut economically from a table of crown glass.

Another innovative feature of the sash window was the method of fixing the glass into the glazing bars with linseed oil putty. That this material was unfamiliar in 1686 is clear from an account given by the Swedish architect Nicodemus Tessin of a visit, in that year, to William III's palace of Het Loo, in Holland. Describing the newly installed sashes, he notes that the glass '. . . is not fixed with lead but with *a substance.*'

It will be appreciated therefore that the last half of the seventeenth century had witnessed something of a revolution in window design. By the early eighteenth century a whole generation of architects and craftsmen had grown up to regard the sash as the usual sort of window, and it is against this background that the development of the fanlight must be considered. This point needs to be stressed because, later in the century, lead was reintroduced into the manufacture of fan-lights, and the use of this material has led, in recent years, to a false association between fanlight making and the earlier leaded-light and stained glass tradition.

The genesis of the fanlight would seem to have been the round-headed version of the sash window in which a logical division into panes of roughly equal size, and the introduction of a door into the lower part of the opening, results in what might be called a proto-fanlight. From such a beginning it is a short step to one of the most common of all timber fanlight designs (Fig. 1).

A constructional refinement, introduced quite early, was to reverse the usual position of the glazing bars so that the mouldings faced outwards, presenting their best face to the side from which they were usually seen. This refinement was not confined to fanlights but was applied also to the windows of shopfronts, which were, similarly, intended to be viewed from the street, nor was it applied universally.

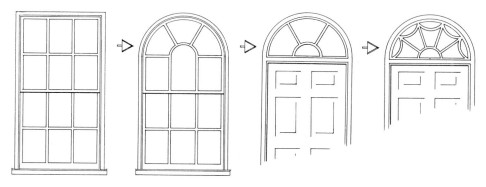

Fig. 1 Possible development of fanlight from sash window

*The simple fretted fanlight of 1724 at Marble Hill House, Twicken-
ham, north front.*

At Papplewick Hall near Nottingham, for instance, the fanlight mouldings face inwards, presumably because it was felt that they would contribute more to the spectacular oval entrance hall than to the rather severe facade.

Roughly contemporary with the development of these window-derived fanlights is a second type, also made in timber, in which the glazed openings are fretted out. A useful example (useful because it is illustrated in Vol.III of *Vitruvius Britannicus* and can, therefore, be securely dated to 1724) is the fanlight over the front entrance to Marble Hill House, Twickenham (above). The fretted fanlight seems to have been a relatively short-lived type and examples are rarely encountered dated later than the 1720s.

As early as the 1730s English architecture had taken a turn towards the whimsi-cal, and a demand for fanlights in fanciful designs (such as those in Castle Street, Farnham; see page 81) which were difficult to execute in wood. Some fifteen years later an interest in improving the view through windows had prompted experi-ments into the use of slim metal glazing bars, and although less concerned with outlook than with a facility for producing curves and ornament, the earliest metal fanlights may be roughly contemporary. They were certainly installed, by (Sir) Robert Taylor, at 35 & 36 Lincoln's Inn Fields in 1755-7, but whether of brass, lead or iron cannot be determined because the last surviving house of the pair was destroyed by bombing in 1941.

Many authorities have claimed that cast iron was the usual material for metal fanlights, but close examination usually reveals timber or some form of composite construction. Although it is quite possible to cast a fanlight in one piece if the glazing bars have the same robust profile as wood, practical difficulties arise when a degree of delicacy is attempted because the glazing webs become so very thin. In practice, cast iron fanlights are either fairly simple in design or else they lack glazing webs and form a decorative grille in front of the glass. Freed from the necessity of linking several panes of glass together, these grilles may be very fanciful indeed (see below).

Although no precise date can be given for its invention, the most common sort of metal fanlight, throughout the later Georgian period, was made from glazing bars of composite lead and iron construction. They were introduced before 1770 because several occur in a group of houses in Grafton Street, again designed by Sir Robert Taylor, and built between 1768 and 1775. In No.4 the entrance hall is divided from the staircase by a screen of Doric columns, and Taylor fills the space above it with a semi-elliptical fanlight fully twelve feet in width, suggesting some confidence in what can hardly have been a novel method of construction. Despite the spectacular size of this screen-light, Taylor's fanlight designs are generally conservative, and it is Robert Adam's influence that is discernable in the profusion of applied

Ashford Road, Tenterden, Kent. What appears to be an intricate fanlight is a cast-iron grille in front of the glass. Such complexity of design would hardly be possible in a multi-paned fanlight.

Construction

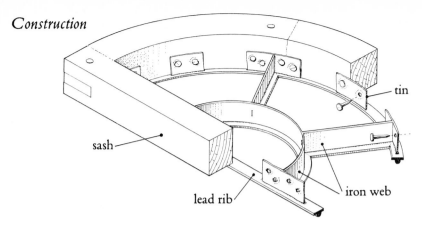

sash

tin

lead rib

iron web

Fig. 2 Construction of a lead-iron fanlight, seen from inside. The glass rests on the lip formed by the lead and is retained by wedges of putty.

ornament that became so characteristic of the 1780s and 90s, and for which lead was such a suitable medium.

From studies involving the cross-matching of cast lead ornaments, it can be shown that most lead-iron fanlights emanated from the firm of Underwood, Bottomley & Hamble of High Holborn, or its successors, Underwood & Doyle and Joseph Bottomley. Although based in London, their products, which included staircase balusters, balcony fronts and skylights, as well as fanlights, were sent to all parts of the country, and exported to America. The technique used, if not evolved, by this firm involved compound glazing bars in which thin webs of tinned wrought iron were soldered to decorative ribs of cast lead. Junctions between glazing bars were soldered, and sometimes reinforced by thin strips of tin. Other strips of tin, crudely tacked to the timber, secured the bars to the sash and supported the peripheral leadwork (Fig. 2). Fanlights made in this way are strong when glazed, because the glass prevents the glazing bars from bending sideways, and durable provided that water does not penetrate the tinning and rust the iron webs. They are also versatile, with a range of basic patterns that can be almost infinitely varied by soldering on cast lead ornaments.

Another successful firm, whose fanlights can be found throughout the country, was the Eldorado Metal & Wrought Iron Sash Co., of Gerrard Street, Soho. Their technique was similar to Underwood and Bottomley's but, instead of lead ribs soldered on, they employed grooved ribs, of malleable cast iron, which were crimped to the glazing webs (Fig. 3), whilst the periphery was finished with a slim

Fig. 3 Comparative sections of glazing bars, about half size: (a) early eighteenth-century window; (b) mid eighteenth-century fanlight; (c) laminated type of mid eighteenth-century fanlight; (d) lead-iron fanlight; (e) Eldorado fanlight, late eighteenth-century; (f) Regency 'lamb's tongue' fanlight; (g) leaded light.

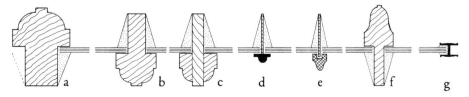

a   b   c   d   e   f   g

Eldorado fanlight from Bridge Street, Worcester, stripped ready for repair and reglazing.

timber moulding pinned to the sash. Additional ornaments were cast in brass and soldered in place. The greater strength of cast iron and brass allowed the number of panes of glass to be reduced and permitted more unsupported ornament, so that Eldorado fanlights tend to be lighter and more spidery than the lead-iron type (see above). With three different materials involved they must always have been painted, whereas the option of a natural finish, only rarely exercised, remained with the Underwood & Bottomley pattern.

If lead and iron had become, by the end of the eighteenth century, the most commonly used materials in the manufacture of ornamental fanlights, fanlights were also made from a variety of other materials. The very fine example, designed by Robert Adam, for 20 St James's Square (shown on page 41) is executed in wrought copper, but this is exceptional and must have been expensive both in materials and workmanship. A more economical method, much used by James Adam in the 1770s, was to enrich a timber fanlight with ornaments made of 'compo', a patent composition, consisting chiefly of whiting and glue, commonly used for the decorations on fireplaces, mirrors and such-like. Outdoors it survived quite well, if properly painted, and was adequately strong when cast around an armature of wire or wrought iron (see pages 54-5).

Almost as this book was going to press a fanlight in South Kensington, dating from about 1840, was discovered to have glazing bars fabricated from a strip of thin zinc sheet rolled into a profile indistinguishable—until paint and putty are stripped away—from the more usual lead-iron examples. Rolling such a form will have required some investment in time and machinery, and there must, therefore, be many other examples of this material as yet undetected. Technically zinc does not seem to offer any advantages over sheet brass or tin, and was probably chosen because it had only recently been introduced as a building material and was enjoying the sort of popularity accorded to 'bakelite' in the 1930s and plastics today.

Repair

It would be impossible, in a chapter of this length, to provide a manual for the restoration and repair of eighteenth-century fanlights, but some repairs can be undertaken at home, and it is to building owners that this section is dedicated, in the hope that they, or their builders, shall avoid some of the more usual problems.

Being confronted with an elderly and slightly tatty fanlight, much of its detail obscured by two hundred years of paint, raises difficult questions about the merits of restoration and originality. Broken glass is not, of course, acceptable, but may not over-painting and a few missing ornaments be part of its period character? Or should it all be carefully cleaned and restored to its original condition? The answers to these questions will vary from owner to owner, depending on their particular philosophy, but it would be a pity if every fanlight was robbed of the patina of age, and the recent revival of interest in historic buildings has, undoubtedly, led to a good deal of needless renewal in the name of restoration. So far as fanlights are concerned, if it is substantially complete and the paintwork is acceptable, it is best left alone, but if elements are missing or the over-painting is too awful to be borne, restoration should be considered. Even then beware, because removing the paint may expose unseen defects, the extent and likelihood of which will depend on the original method of construction.

Before deciding which course to take it is, then, advisable to identify the type of fanlight and to make a preliminary survey of its condition and, should the worst befall, how the sash could be removed from the doorcase. First of all make sure that it really is a proper fanlight, made up of a number of separate panes of glass secured by wedges of putty, and not a leaded light or some recent confection applied to a sheet of plate glass. Timber fanlights are easily recognised by their relatively robust construction, but any doubts can be dispelled by touch. Very slim bars, such that the putty forms a sharp Vee, also indicate metal, and the two main types of metal fanlight can be distinguished by their borders; if the peripheral ribs are complete, and stand proud of the sash, it is by one of the lead-iron makers, but if they are half ribs, set just below the level of the sash, it comes from the Eldorado factory.

Because timber fanlights are relatively robust, and any defects can be remedied by a competent joiner, detailed examination can be reserved for the metal types. Eldorado lights are stronger but missing ornaments are expensive to replace because they are cast in brass, so a note should be made of any absent detail and whether it is repeated elsewhere in the design, for possible use as a pattern. Distorted ornaments should not be straightened because the alloy seems to become crystalline and brittle with age; lead is more forgiving in this respect. The same inventory should be made for a fanlight by one of the lead-iron makers, but with these it is more important to check the condition of the external border and the internal glazing bars. If the lead border is badly distorted, or fractured, some restoration will be inevitable if the existing paint is removed, and if the insides of the glazing bars show signs of rusting away, the cost of restoration will probably exceed the price of a replica. If these conditions are observed, and expense is a consideration, the advice of a specialist should be sought.

A lead-iron fanlight cannot be parted from its sash, so if restoration is favoured, the whole unit will have to be removed to the restorer's workshop, and the implications of this should be taken into account when making the final decision; for instance, will the removal of the sash cause irreparable damage to decorative plasterwork or panelling? Or is it feasible to remove it at all, without breaking it, bearing in mind that the bottom member is likely to have been weakened by water penetration? Eighteenth-century sashes are usually fixed by a few, rather large, cut nails. Their heads are punched below the surface and the hole filled with putty. To remove the sash these nails must first be found and then, since they cannot be extracted, punched right through the sash into the door frame or whatever. This is not always as simple as it sounds.

The alternative to restoring an original fanlight is to build a new one, and, provided that it is well done, there does not seem to be any very valid argument against it, since restoration itself will destroy the only feature that cannot be replicated, namely the patina of age, and there are several advantages to building anew: the troublesome iron armature can be replaced by rust resistant metal, construction can be improved—some early nineteenth-century fanlights were very shoddily built—and, although it is always preferable to build into a new sash, it is possible to build a self-supporting fanlight for insertion into an original sash where, for the reasons indicated above, it cannot be removed to the workshop.

It remains to describe those repairs which can be attempted in situ: reglazing, certainly, and, subject to the caveats above, stripping and repainting, and the replacing of missing ornaments.

The most common repair will be renewing a pane of glass, but, although this should not be beyond anyone having a degree of competence with a glass cutter, the greatest risk to the fanlight comes from removing the old glass and putty, particularly when lead is involved in the construction, because old putty is much harder than lead. Putty should, therefore, be softened before removal by applying a poultice of 'Ronstrip' to the margins of the damaged pane and leaving it for a day or two, covered in polythene to prevent evaporation. With a lead-iron fanlight, check that no external ornaments are so bound up with paint and putty that they are likely to come away with the old glass. If they are, it may be advisable to apply some stripper to the outside, even though this could end in having to remove all the old paint.

Whilst the putty is softening a search can be made for some suitable glass. Modern window glass is too flat and characterless and is only tolerable in very small panes. James Hetley & Co. (for address see page 29) supply a crown glass substitute which gives a fair imitation of the liveliness of early glass, but without the slight concentric ripples associated with genuine crown. Alternatively the cheaper sort of horticultural glass, especially the glass imported from Russia, is sufficiently flawed and distorted to pass for eighteenth-century broad sheet. If the fanlight contains areas of coloured glass this can also be obtained from Hetley's, but only in flat sheet. However, because the areas of colour are usually quite small, this does not seem to matter. The stock colours are Pot Amber, Pot Blue and Pot Red.

The new glass is cut to a pattern made by holding a piece of card against the back of the glazing bars and tracing round the opening with a felt-tipped pen (most felt-tips make a line just broad enough to give a nice working clearance when the centre of the line is followed by the cutter). The pattern is laid under the glass and the line retraced with a wheeled cutter, using moderate pressure and steady forward motion, because glass responds well when the cutter is used smoothly and with confidence. The best cutters have a small knob at the end of the handle which is used to start the cut by tapping the back of the wheel mark. The cut may then be continued by tapping, or made to run by laying the glass, face down, on an old piece of carpet and pressing the tapping knob on the back of the scored line.

After checking that the glass fits, it is bedded in a little multi-purpose putty and finished off neatly inside with a narrow wedge against the glazing bars. The secret of a neat finish lies in a well polished knife and the consistency of the putty, which should be as firm as possible. Bought putty is far too soft, but it can be stiffened by keeping it warm whilst rolled out onto brown paper, which absorbs some of the oils. If the glazing bars are curved a narrow putty knife is needed, and a suitable tool can be made by grinding off the end of an old kitchen knife. For work next to the sash the blade needs to be angled, but this can only be done at red heat.

To remove paint with 'Ronstrip' the same technique is used as described above for softening putty. When treating a whole fanlight in this way it is a good idea to cut, out of a sheet of thick polythene, a piece a few inches larger than the sash, plus a few extra inches at the bottom. This is firmly pinned over the fanlight with a loop at the bottom to catch any lumps of stripper and drips of softened paint, which might otherwise fall onto the heads and clothes of unwary visitors. 'Ronstrip' contains caustic soda and should never be used on timber fanlights with compo ornaments, nor should such fanlights be sent away for cleaning since the ornaments will dissolve away entirely in the caustic baths used by commercial pine and door stripping companies. Paint can be removed from compo with a jelly stripper such as 'Nitromors' provided that its progress is carefully monitored and any excess stripper removed, with white spirit and cotton wool, as soon as the compo shows through. A safe solvent is cellulose thinner; unfortunately it is flammable, and evaporates so rapidly that it is almost impossible to use in situ, but it can be used to clean up detached ornaments intended for use as patterns.

When a leaded fanlight has been stripped of its many layers of paint, revealing the delicacy of some of the castings, the temptation to leave it unpainted must be resisted. Because they originated in the timber sash-window tradition nearly all fanlights were originally painted to match the surrounding woodwork. Unpainted examples can be found, but they are rare and usually confined to doorcases of polished hardwood. When stripping an old fanlight it will often be noticed that the soldered joints are brighter than the rest of the leadwork, and, because solder assumes the same colour as lead within a few weeks of exposure, this demonstrates very neatly that it has always been painted.

There is no paint especially suitable for lead—in fact paint manufacturers recommend that it be left unpainted—but ordinary oil-based paints seem to adhere quite well, and, given a good primer, have proved quite satisfactory in the past. Red lead primers provide a suitable background for dark colours whilst the covering power of white or cream finishes is assisted by the excellent International Metal Primer intended for use on central heating radiators.

In a workshop restoration, missing ornaments would be replaced, of course, in their original materials. With metal fanlights this involves resoldering which cannot be done with the glass in place or without removing all the paint. For in situ repairs, however, and since the ornaments will be painted anyway, it is easier and safer to replace them in a resin-based casting medium. Resins also have the advan-tage of not shrinking and, therefore, yield perfect copies of the pattern: to produce the same result in cast lead involves carving a wooden pattern 5 per cent larger than the original ornament. There are several compounds available, but Belzona Moul-dable Wood is convenient because it can be mixed to a flowing consistency ideal for pouring into a mould.

Because two of the most readily obtained materials for making a simple mould (plaster of Paris and plasticine) are unsuitable for use with resins, it will be necessary to obtain a quantity of one of the moulding materials used by sculptors. For metal patterns 'Vinamould' is the quickest and most convenient to use and the softer, red, variety should be chosen. It is poured molten and should not be used on compo, which is susceptible to heat. Alternatively, the mould could be made from one of the cold curing silicone rubbers, such as RTV11, which are every bit as effective as Vinamould but take longer to cure.

Whichever material is chosen the pattern, that is an undamaged ornament or a plaster cast of one, is fixed to a sheet of plywood with double-sided Sellotape, and a small box or fence built around it (in the case of silicone rubber the pattern is best fixed to glass, while 'Lego' makes an ideal fence). The moulding material, heated or mixed according to the supplier's directions, is poured slowly into the mould until the whole pattern is covered; air bubbles are less likely to be trapped if it is poured alongside, not onto, the pattern, so that the material flows over it gradually. When set the box is removed and the mould gently peeled off. A quantity of Belzona is then mixed and poured in, slightly over-filling the mould. After five or ten minutes, to allow time for air bubbles to escape but before the resin hardens, place a sheet of shiny card (cereal packet is fine) on top, followed by a flat block of wood and any convenient weight. This squeezes out excess resin, giving a smooth back to the cast, whilst the card prevents the resin from adhering to the wood. The completed ornament is washed in cellulose thinners, to remove any stickiness, and fixed with 'Araldite', but if the back of the ornament can be seen from inside, and the glass is already in place, remember to paint the visible rear section before fixing.

Suppliers in UK of specialist items mentioned: *Glass*: James Hetley & Co Ltd, Beresford Avenue, Wembley, Middx. HA0 1RP; *Moulding materials*: Alec Tiranti Ltd, 70 High Street, Theale, Berks. RG7 5AR; *Belzona mouldable wood*: Belzona Molecular Ltd, Claro Road, Harro-gate, N. Yorks. HG1 4AY. (Ronstrip, Nitromors, Araldite and the various paints can be obtained from any good hardware or DIY shop.)

Glossary

Acanthus A plant having large spiny leaves represented in the decoration of capitals of the Corinthian and Composite orders and of other parts of the ORDER. The Greeks copied the pointed variety, the Romans the rounded.

Anthemion Representations of the honeysuckle flower occurred in the art and architecture of ancient Greece and were adopted by the Romans.

Arabesque Low relief of painted decoration representing flowers, fruit or geometric patterns following Moslem observance.

Arch A construction, semicircular, elliptical, segmental, or OGEE, built up of wedge-shaped blocks called voussoirs.

Architrave The lowest member of the ENTABLATURE. Also the same moulding when carried down the sides of a door or fireplace or down the sides and under the sill of a window. When carried round the EXTRADOS of an ARCH it is called an archivolt.

Archivolt see ARCHITRAVE.

Ashlar Masonry worked to prescribed shapes and sizes and carved or moulded *before* setting in the work. In America it is known as hewn stone.

Astragal A small convex moulding. Also the glazing bead of a window moulded on both sides with such a moulding.

Casement Window An unspecific term describing a window where the opening parts are *hinged*.

Clapboarding The long narrow strips of wood of tapered section nailed horizontally, overlapping, to protect the outside of timber-framed building (in England: weatherboarding).

Composite Order see ORDER.

Console A bracket in the form of a scroll supporting a CORNICE.

Corinthian Order see ORDER.

Cornice The top member of an ENTABLATURE or such a member occurring alone.

Cross-window The window composed of four leaded lights in iron sashes set in a wood frame, mullion and TRANSOM which form a cross, fitted to classical buildings (*viz* the Banquetting House, Whitehall, London) before the arrival of the SASH WINDOW from Holland.

Cyma Recta or *Cymatium* A moulding comprising a concave curve above a convex curve, or the top member of the sloping sides of a PEDIMENT, also the top member of a horizontal CORNICE where there is no pediment.

Cyma Reversa A moulding composed of two quarter-round curves, the upper convex, the lower concave.

Dentil The tooth-like ornament cut out of a plain square moulding.

Doric Order see ORDER.

Engaged Column A column appearing to be partly embedded in the wall behind it, leaving *over half* of its circumference exposed.

Entablature The upper part of an order comprising ARCHITRAVE, FRIEZE and CORNICE (see ORDER).

Fascia The horizontal band (usually) of an ARCHITRAVE.

Festoon A festive garland or swag represented in stone, wood or plaster, or painted; or in metal, where it represents chains of beads or husks, as in metal fanlights.

Fluting The concave grooves running up a column or PILASTER. When, in the lower third of a column or pilaster, a convex moulding fills the fluting, it is known as cabled fluting.

Frieze That part of an ENTABLATURE between the ARCHITRAVE and the CORNICE. When given a convex or OGEE cushion profile it is called a pulvinated frieze.

Fret A moulding enriched by plain bands interlocking to form a continuous chain, either of square shapes or round links.

Gothick The spelling used in this book to indicate the pointed and OGEE arched style occurring in the eighteenth century ornamental and garden buildings, as introduced by Horace Walpole.

Guilloche The cursive interlacing pattern enriching a moulding or FRIEZE.

Guttae The pegs carved below each TRIGLYPH recalling the timber origin of the first Greek temples.

Hewn Stone see ASHLAR.

Impost The moulding from which an arch springs.

Ionic Order see ORDER.

Metope The square panel in a FRIEZE of the Greek and Roman Doric orders, often, as in the Parthenon, Athens, filled with sculpture.

Modillion A bracket, plain or scrolled, under the corona of a CORNICE.

Ogee The profile of a moulding or of an ARCH comprising two opposing curves.

Order The column base, shaft, capital and ENTABLATURE designed in accordance with certain rules first set down by the Roman military architect Marcus Vitruvius Pollio, and re-affirmed by the Italian architect Sebastian Serlio (1475–1554). *Greek :* Doric, Ionic, Corinthian. *Roman :* Doric, Tuscan, Ionic, Corinthian, Composite.

Ovolo A convex moulding based upon the quarter of an ellipse or of a circle.

Palladian Window (Also called a Venetian window.) A window three lights wide, having the centre light arched and the side lights spanned by a lintel. Introduced first by the Italian architect Andrea Palladio (1508–80) in Vincenza.

Palmette Decoration resembling a palm leaf.

Patera A circular disc ornament in the form of a shield or of a rose, when it is called a rosette.

Pediment The triangular, segmental or otherwise shaped finish to a gable or, in miniature, over a door, window or other architectural feature. Composed of the CORNICE of the ENTABLATURE crowned by the CYMATIUM (which does *not* appear across the base chord of the triangle or segment).
  Open pediment : Where the inclined or curved sides terminate before they meet.
  Broken pediment : Where the horizontal base is interrupted to allow penetration by an ARCH.

Curved pediment : Where the sloping sides form a segmental curve.

Pilaster A flat pier carrying the base, capital, fluting and ENTABLATURE of the ORDER to which it belongs.

Reveal The vertical side of an opening in a wall.

Rosette see PATERA.

Rustication Blocks in an ASHLAR stone wall either bevelled or carved to simulate rough stone blocks, or with a pattern such as VERMICULATION. Also alternate blocks in a column PILASTER or ARCHITRAVE either rusticated or plain.

'Sash' Window The colloquial term for a window consisting of 'double-hung vertical sliding sashes in cased frames', introduced into England from Holland during the reign of William III and Queen Mary after 1689. Correctly, the 'sash' is the inner frame holding the glass, sliding, hinged or fixed.

Soffit(e) The underside of a lintel.

Spandrel or *Spandril* The spaces left between a circle or semicircle and the square space it occupies, occurring usually around an ARCH.

Swag see FESTOON.

Tabernacle Window A window decorated with a pair of columns or PILASTERS supporting an ENTABLATURE with or without a PEDIMENT.

Transom The horizontal bar separating two parts of window, or separating a door from its fanlight. In America sometimes referring to the fanlight as well.

Triglyph Blocks in the FRIEZE of the Doric ORDER carved with two and two half channels, said to represent the timber origin of the first temples.

Tuscan Order see ORDER.

Venetian Window see PALLADIAN WINDOW.

Vermiculation Artificial worm like pattern on the face of stone. see RUSTICATION.

Volute The spiral scroll on the capitals of the Ionic and Corinthian and Composite ORDERS.

Voussoirs see ARCH.

Weatherboarding see CLAPBOARDING .

The beautiful lights at 88 and 90 High Street, Islington,
resemble the early 'chair-back' designs at Farnham,
Surrey (see page 80); they are yet more rococo.

London

The practice throughout the towns and cities of Great Britain and Ireland of living in separate houses, however grand, however mean, astonished visitors to those islands, among them Voltaire. Sir John Summerson, in his *Georgian London*, quotes from Voltaire's *Journal of a Tour and Residence in Great Britain, 1817* Vol.1:

> *The narrow houses, three or four storeys high, one for eating, one for sleeping, a third for company, a fourth underground for the kitchen, a fifth, perhaps at the top, for the servants, and the agility, the ease, the quickness with which the individuals of the family run up and down and perch on the different storeys, give the idea of a cage with its sticks and birds.*

How did this belt of terraced houses develop around our towns and cities? Who built them? Who paid for them? And upon whose land were they built? Expansion beyond the city's fortifications was possible in Britain centuries before such escape could be achieved in the cities of Europe. In London soon to emerge out of Ludgate and to cross the Fleet Ditch and settle beyond the monastery of Black Friars were the lawyers, the Earls of Norfolk, Somerset, Exeter, York, Northumberland and Lancaster. They had settled along the Thames when the river was the chief means of communication.

In the seventeenth century a start was made towards further expansion; a speculator who had built for the lawyers in their Inns of Court set his sights upon land north of Holborn and had started to build. Whether or not this activity by Nicholas Barbon sparked off a movement to acquire land for building towards the northern heights of London and west towards the old Roman Watling Street (Edgware Road), such a movement was made by the ducal families, by the Church of England, by the Colleges of Eton and Harrow and Rugby, while the City Companies and Charities directed their attention northwards and eastwards.

The object of the extensive acquisition of land was, of course, for investment—for ground rents and the subsequent reversion after a lease of sixty or ninety-nine years of the houses. How were these landowners to get houses built to a plan of reasonable orderliness and at the least outlay for themselves? For a peppercorn rent they would grant to a small master builder several plots of land. The builder would sell the houses to new owners who would become leaseholders of the house and land. During the term agreed the ground landlord or his successors would receive a substantial income, and at the end of the term, the land and the houses would return to them. Usually the builder would employ only the bricklayers, carpenters and tilers. The purchaser of the house would employ directly joiners and plasterers to complete the carcase. In the absence of public support only this method would enable the thousands needing homes to find accommodation, for most of the houses were rented out by those who purchased them in blocks.

Not only the Great Fire of 1666 but migration from the provinces and from Europe had increased the size of London until it was nicknamed 'The Great Wen' by William Cobbett (1763-1835). The inner parishes of London had been filling up. In the seventeenth century Charles II had granted a lease in St James's to Henry Jermyn, the Duke of St Albans, where he developed St James's Square and Street, Jermyn Street and the streets around. In Clerkenwell, where under James I Sir Hugh Myddleton had brought fresh water from Hertfordshire to London, the New River Estate was built up, and next to it the Lloyd-Baker Estate, and south of it the Earl of Northampton's Estate. The building of Westminster Bridge, Southwark Bridge and Blackfriars Bridge encouraged building south of the river beyond Southwark to Kennington.

The first to build north of the Strand had been the fourth Earl of Bedford, who had instructed Inigo Jones to design a square for him on former monastic land—Covent Garden. His heirs pushed the Bedford Estates as far as the New Road. West, beyond St Martin's Lane, came Soho Square, next came Hanover Square, a Whig venture. Beyond, the Grosvenor Estate began to develop, enlarged by the marriage between a Grosvenor and Mary Davies, the heiress to the land in the angle between Hyde Park and Oxford Street, now the richest estate in London. At the same time Lord Burlington was developing his land north of his house in Piccadilly.

North of Oxford Street there was more room for building. The fields owned by the Fitzroy family, by the Dukes of Portland, by the Cavendish-Harley family and by the Portmans, stretched as far as Marylebone Fields, crossed in 1760 by the New Road from Paddington to Islington. At first the new building did not carry as far as that, until John Nash laid out the Fields for the Prince Regent as Regent's Park, connecting it to Portland Place with Park Square and Park Crescent.

The management of each of the estates was conducted by the estate surveyor or agent. Not always was an architect called in, for the types of houses and their construction were laid down by Parliament. The Building Act of 1774 laid down standards for terraced houses which were designated First, Second, Third and Fourth class. As a fire precaution, the Building Acts of 1707 and 1709 had prohibited the external crowning wood cornice which had been the standard since the Fire of 1666, and insisted instead upon a parapet at the head of the front wall. As a further precaution against the spread of fire externally, the Acts required the box frames of the 'sash' windows to be set back and hidden behind four inches of brickwork. This accounts for a noticeable difference between the façade of a 'Queen Anne' house and a 'Georgian' house.

In the second half of the eighteenth century a change of taste occurred in the south of England in the choice of bricks. The 'stock' brick—that is the clamp⁄ burnt rough brick—had been burnt from clays which gave a dark red⁄brown colour. Owing to the strong influence of the Adam brothers, who had come from the stone country of Edinburgh, and also largely to the work at Bath in brown limestone (Bath Stone) by the John Woods, father and son, and to the imitation of Bath Stone, the red⁄brown brick went out of fashion in London, where it was replaced by the yellow brick referred to after as the 'London Stock'.

Soon Bath stone itself made its appearance in London. How did Bath stone make this journey? Portland Stone had always been brought by sea, but owing to the near impossibility of bringing stone from the Bath district round Land's End, it did not appear in any quantity in London until after the opening of the Kennet and Avon Canal in 1810.

The leasing of plots for houses on the Portland and Portman estates to Robert and James Adam gave them the opportunity of showing their work and, if not designed by them, many houses there showed their influence. And so this area of north⁄west London became the seed⁄bed of the 'Adam fanlight' and the origin of the term fanlight.

As we have seen, designs in the true fan shape appeared in pattern books and soon in the catalogues of the manufacturers. The true fan⁄shaped fanlight was not confined to houses of the first and second class. North and east of the City, estates were built in Islington and Hackney where there was a need for the smaller house, houses of the third and fourth class—a door and *one* window in width. These too had often an arched door. Due in part to the problems of getting large sheets of glass, partly to give some elegance to the house, a fanlight was inserted. Being smaller, it was often in a simple geometric arrangement of wooden glazing bars, but some⁄ times in an ingenious and imaginative design in iron and lead, as many of the drawings which follow show.

When the Greek style followed the interest in the remains of the buildings of Ancient Greece, the severe lines of that trabeated style required the elimination of the arch from the front door and the rectangular fanlight became *de rigueur*. This often took the form of a series of rounded oblongs which suited the severe lines of the channelled stucco base of the wall. Sometimes the 'fan' motif persisted and an arch drawn in metal within the rectangle was fitted out with the fan design which had become traditional.

The following pages illustrate the variety of fanlight designs which are found in London. The sequence is regional, conforming in large measure to the develop⁄ ment of the great estates. It is not chronological and the designs are very varied, with some shapes appearing unexpectedly as a result of later insertion. However, the rich variety of London fanlights is clearly shown.

RIGHT *A large replica fanlight, made by John Sambrook, in Mecklenburgh Square, London WC1.*

ABOVE   *At 30 John Street, London WC1 is the simplest of all wood overdoor designs based on the window heads of the period. Compare with 9 Queen Anne's Gate (see page 6).*

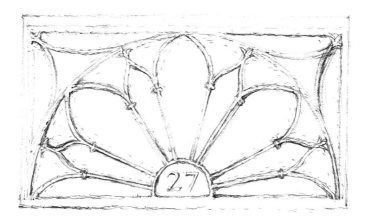

27 & 28 Great James Street, London WC1. No. 27 is a pretty example of the possibilities of paired spokes. Each is a nineteenth-century metal insertion in an earlier doorframe.

LEFT   *36 Catherine Place, London SW1. We have here the sweetest possible example of the arched doorway with fanlight intercepting a pediment supported upon the slenderest of entablatures.*

ABOVE *Rectangular fanlights at 2 & 9 Bedford Row, London WC1. No. 9 is a curious 'batswing' design : where the batswings enfold the central house number they resemble angels' wings.*

BELOW *Symmetrical fanlights in Dombey Street, London WC1. No. 12 has a roundel for the house number, and at No. 11* BOTTOM *there are floral ornaments at the nodal points.*

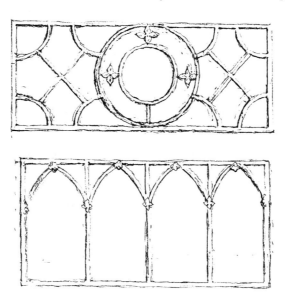

TOP *10 Downing Street, London SW1. This restored fanlight of six spokes linked by arches is of early date. The spandrels were originally glazed.* ABOVE *At 11 Downing Street, the official residence of the Chancellor of the Exchequer, a graceful figure is produced in the fanlight by the intersection of two semicircles, two segments and two ogee curves, creating between them eleven panes of six different shapes.*

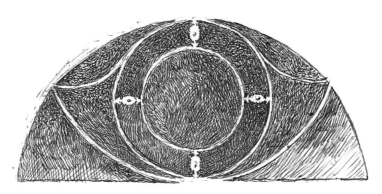

Many of the fanlights in Trevor Square, Knightsbridge, are of teardrop pattern. At No. 36 ABOVE *a double circle to contain the house number is held between a pair of slings. Not far away, the Edwardian architecture of Harrods incorporates a row of Art Nouveau fanlights into the first-floor windows.*

39

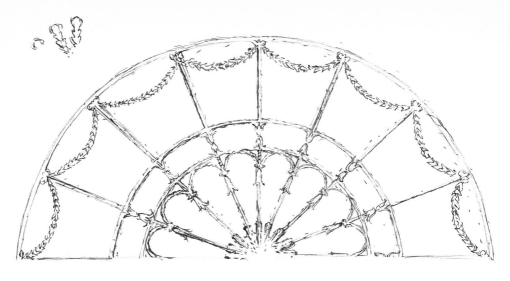

Adam influence is evident in the Grosvenor Estate, London W1. ABOVE *The delicate fanlight at* 19
Albemarle Street, the premises of W. H. Patterson Ltd, Fine Art. BELOW *Seven circles between the*
spokes and double arch rings provide the main theme at 10 *Hill Street.* BOTTOM *The rectangular fanlight*
at the offices of John Murray, Publisher, 50 *Albemarle Street, symmetrical about two axes. A rectangle*
encloses an oval in a design that would serve as a ceiling pattern in the Adam style.

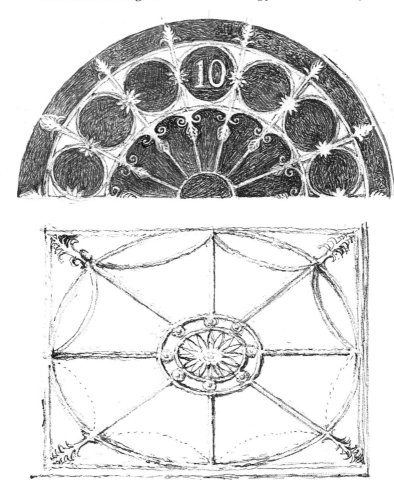

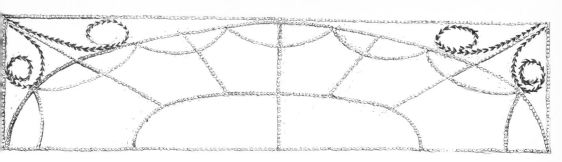

ABOVE *This wide fanlight spans the interior of an historic shop at No. 34 Haymarket, London SW1. The shop was established in the eighteenth century by the tobacconists Evans & Evans, whose business was continued until recently by Fribourg & Treyer. The interior fanlight crowned a late eighteenth-century screen which divided the outer shop with its counters and assistants from the inner sanctum where the proprietors would receive favoured customers.* BELOW *Robert Adam designed No. 20 St James's Square, London SW1, for Sir Watkin Williams-Wynne between 1772 and 1774.* BOTTOM *At 20 Upper Berkeley Street, London W1, once the home of Dr Elizabeth Garrett Anderson, England's first woman doctor, the Adam-style fanlight includes lily flowers and beaded loops, as shown in the detail.*

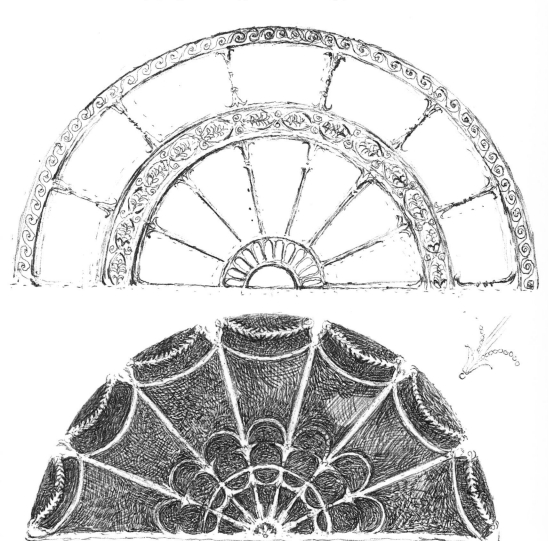

The Portman Estate, London W1 and NW1, contains many fine metal fanlights, illustrated on this and the
following seven pages. Typical is No. 19 Montagu Street ABOVE with rosettes in a double band. At 49 Great
Cumberland Place, BELOW the band contains four-petalled flowers, and the spokes spring from an unusual sunburst.

*Several houses in Great Cumberland Place have fanlights. No.51 ABOVE has
a teardrop on either side of a circle contained within margins of linked diamonds.*

Montagu Square, London W1, provides contrasts. ABOVE *An intricate design by Bottomley, at No. 25, with festoons and garlands. Unfortunately much of the decoration is now lost. At No. 34* BELOW *is a simple but subtle design of intersecting circles, within a semicircle, set within a segmental frame. The fanlights at Nos. 21, 46* BOTTOM *and 49 are of the same pattern, with anthemion (honeysuckle) ornament, as shown in the detail, and a band of twenty-five ovals around the perimeter.*

43

Robert Adam designed No. 21 Portman Square, London W1. His large fanlight ABOVE *has seven spokes. The similar design* BELOW *at 23 Gloucester Place, London W1 has eight, and a band containing stars within circles.*

BELOW *This fanlight at 1 Dorset Square has a style consistently Greek, Greek in its nine groups of three frets around the perimeter, Greek in the double rings of its rays like the corona of Athena.*

At No. 21 Bryanston Square London W1 ABOVE *a series of lozenges link the spokes decorated with garlands. The house is now a Swiss Embassy residence. Between the five spokes of the fan at No. 16* BELOW *is a band of tiny festoons. Under the peripheral double ring, swags holding small rings swing between the spokes. Removed from the extreme periphery, the double semicircle displays its chain of circles and diamonds. The detail drawing illustrates the very tricky junction between six elements of the design.*

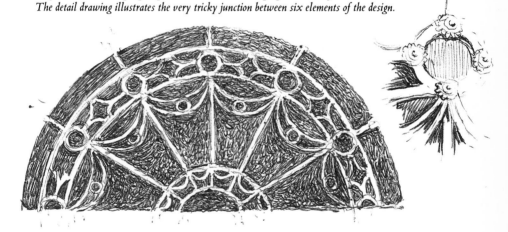

BELOW *No. 31 Gloucester Place (and No. 37, similar) has a chain of diamonds created by a row of arches around the perimeter and another row springing from the spokes. The patera decoration, like a cameo brooch, is illustrated in the detail.*

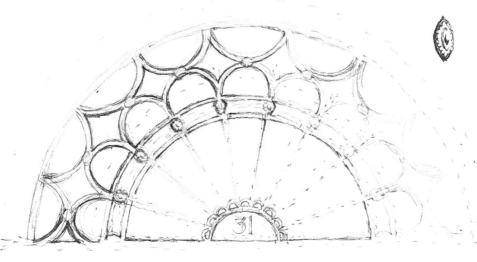

Fine and varied fanlights line both sides of Gloucester Place, London W1 and NW1. At No. 63 OPPOSITE the eight spokes of the fanlight are joined at the perimeter by pointed arches, not as a gothick fantasy but to form a large flower of seven petals. The intermediate hemisphere has a chain of sixteen ovals. The wide single door this fanlight spans is made, as was the fashion towards the end of the eighteenth century, in the form of two leaves meeting at a rebated and headed centre. Next door at No. 65 ABOVE lived for a time William Wilkie Collins, the author of 'The Woman In White'. Here is a fanlight in the true Adam style, ornamented with garlands, tiny capitals and lilies. By contrast, at 195 Gloucester Place BELOW is a single teardrop design containing a circle intended most probably for the house number. At No. 197 BOTTOM the six spokes, connected by seven arches, make a flower form.

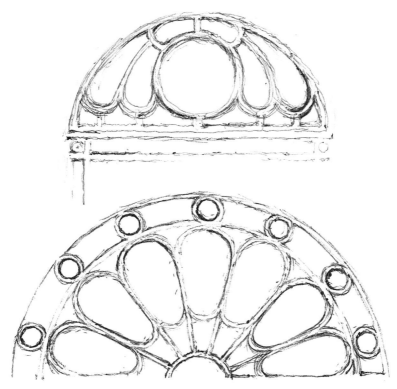

In 1810, at No. 4 Duke Street, London W1 ABOVE stayed Simon Bolivar, liberator of the Spanish colonies in Equatorial South America. The fanlight, although simple, is decorative, relying on the pattern and dispensing with ornament. The true 'fan light' from which the design of overdoor light derives its name can be recognised by its straight ribs, radiating like the spokes of a wheel from the hub until they arrive near the periphery of the arch. However, more organic forms abound, with petals and shells as their inspiration. At 30 Ivor Place, London NW1 BELOW a gentle curving of some of the radial bars converts a fan to a flower. See also the Dublin fanlight on page 125.

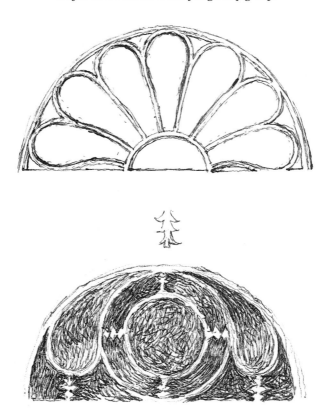

At 29 Ivor Place, London NW1, are two teardrops falling on each side of a medallion. Supporting each 'tear' and separating the two rings of the medallion is a device of bell flowers or husks, as shown in the detail.

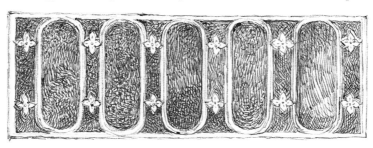

A typical batswing motif is illustrated TOP *at 48 York Street, Marylebone, London NW1. However, the filling of a segmental arch at nearby No. 4 Wyndham Place* ABOVE *by the addition of only four ingeniously placed extra strokes has converted a pattern of nine segments and three circles into an image so ghoulish that approached at night, be it bat or bird, it could be threatening.*

When the form of the house grew more severe the Pompeian style of Robert Adam was replaced by a lintelled style and a simple form of grille filled the overdoor light. The example BELOW *at No. 80 Balcombe Street is typical. An even plainer version is found in several houses in Nash's Park Square* BOTTOM.

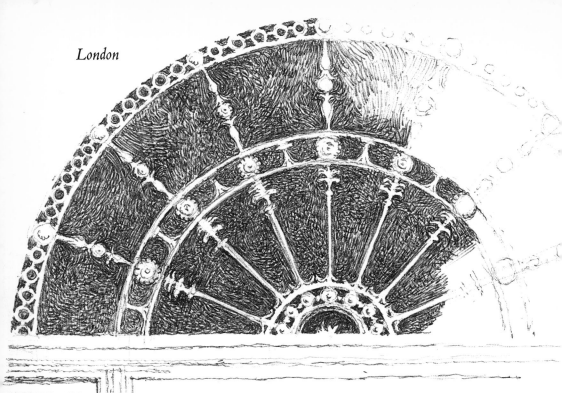

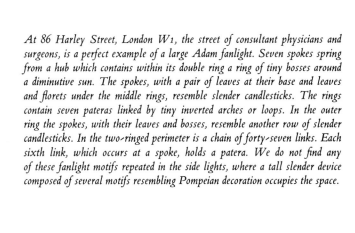

At 86 Harley Street, London W1, the street of consultant physicians and surgeons, is a perfect example of a large Adam fanlight. Seven spokes spring from a hub which contains within its double ring a ring of tiny bosses around a diminutive sun. The spokes, with a pair of leaves at their base and leaves and florets under the middle rings, resemble slender candlesticks. The rings contain seven pateras linked by tiny inverted arches or loops. In the outer ring the spokes, with their leaves and bosses, resemble another row of slender candlesticks. In the two-ringed perimeter is a chain of forty-seven links. Each sixth link, which occurs at a spoke, holds a patera. We do not find any of these fanlight motifs repeated in the side lights, where a tall slender device composed of several motifs resembling Pompeian decoration occupies the space.

Across the wide hallway of 131 Harley Street stretches the fanlight ABOVE separating the outer hall
from the stairway. The orthodox design is distinguished by rare blue glass in the outermost panes above
the festoons, again in the spandrels above the petals, and around the centre of the hub.

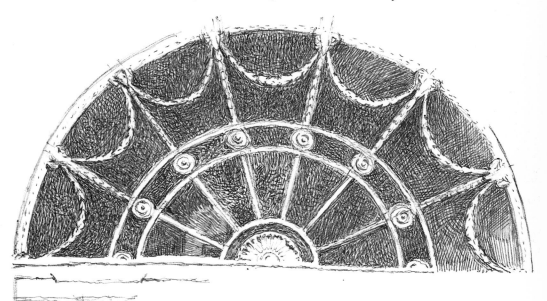

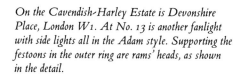

On the Cavendish-Harley Estate is Devonshire
Place, London W1. At No. 13 is another fanlight
with side lights all in the Adam style. Supporting the
festoons in the outer ring are rams' heads, as shown
in the detail.

51

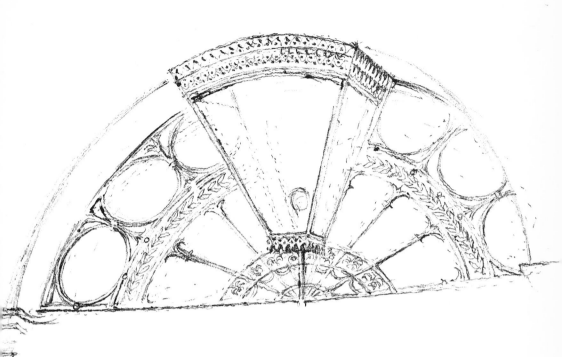

The splendid pair of doorways ABOVE at 46 and 48 Portland Place, London W1 share the same arched porch. They belong to a pair of houses on the east side of Portland Place, and the street, then a close, was the widest in London. The width was not determined by convenience but to preserve the view to Marylebone Fields from Foley House, the residence of Lord Foley, where the Langham Hotel stands now. The close became a thoroughfare when John Nash incorporated it into the Prince Regent's grand route from Carlton House on the Mall to the fields which became Regent's Park. The street today presents a lamentable sight. Half the houses built by the brothers Adam have been replaced by buildings showing no regard for the former elegance of the street. Not the first offender, but by no means the least, was the Royal Institute of British Architects. The two doorways stand on a gentle curve so that they turn towards each other, as the drawing shows. Each fanlight holds a large three-sided lantern which fits under the arch.

LEFT No. 1 Upper Wimpole Street, London W1. Whether we call this splendid fanlight a teardrop design or a batswing design depends upon one small detail — the segmental bars missing from the base of the ribs. The centre medallion which holds the house number has eight stars; the peripheral ring has a necklace of sixteen circles decreasing in size towards the top. Compare this with the light at 25 Duncan Terrace, London N1 (page 61) and at 46 Mecklenburgh Square (page 35).

53

The houses in Mansfield Street, London W1 were designed by Robert Adam and built between 1770 and 1775. Only the west side today retains the original houses. At No. 11 BELOW is a fanlight carefully restored and protected by a single sheet of glass. Garlands linking the eight spokes form a corona around the hub which holds the house number. A chain of small rings and large flowers decorates the perimeter – see detail. At No. 15 ABOVE is a splendid fanlight with six spokes doubling to thirteen in the outer ring. The inner circle is more elaborate than usual – two bands of beads surround a chain of links. Between the spokes, pairs of volutes meet to hold lily flowers. All the existing fanlights in Mansfield Street are made of timber and 'compo' (see page 25). Between the two houses whose fanlights are illustrated here

lived the great architect Sir Edwin Lutyens. The original fanlight at No. 13 is missing now, but during Lutyens' life through the fanlight could be seen a plaster bust of the architect wearing a topee and smoking a pipe. Exactly contemporary with Mansfield Street were houses in Grafton Street by Sir Robert Taylor. At No. 5 BELOW the semicircular Adam design is raised on a glazed frieze to form a deep rectangle.

The most successful square on the estate purchased by the Duke of Bedford was Bedford Square, built jointly by Robert Palmer and Thomas Leverton. It was designed with a central pediment on the north and south sides which may have derived from James Adam's Portland Place. All the fanlights in Bedford Square were in the Adam tradition and had swags of festoons between the rams' heads in the outer circle. These do not form part of the glazing web, but were supported in front of the glass by steel wire. Because this rusted away, most of the swags in the square have disappeared, as ABOVE at No. 4. In the fanlight at No. 6 BELOW, reconstructed by John Sambrook, the festoon ornament has been reinstated, so that this fanlight is a more authentic design than its neighbours.

At 29 Tavistock Square, Bloomsbury, London WC1 ABOVE *are two fanlights, one over the street door, the other over an inner lobby door, and of a design more elaborate than delicate. A broad perimeter band is composed of an intricate pattern of large openwork lilies alternating with openwork palmettes, each at the end of a spoke.*

At Nos. 1, 2 and 3 Regent Square, London WC1 BELOW *are identical fanlights which signal a minor revolution in fanlight design. By pairing the twelve spokes and linking them alternately by arches and loops, the image is created of a three-dimensional figure of folds or flutes. They can also give the impression of an aurora or of a sea shell. Where Regent Square succeeds, Lloyd Street, London WC1 BOTTOM fails.*

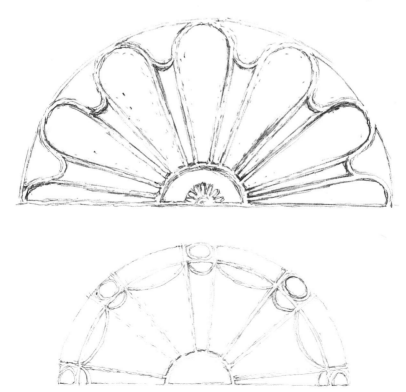

Charlotte Street, London WC1 is on the Southampton Fitzroy Estate, which included the site of Euston Station and Euston Square (Euston being a village in Suffolk on the Fitzroy property). Robert Adam designed Fitzroy Square, and nearby Charlotte Street was named after the consort of George III. The fanlight of No. 26 Charlotte Street ABOVE has a pretty row of fourteen interlacing arches at the perimeter. Where they meet the hemicycle there hang lilies, but some of them have fallen away.

The mood of fanlight can be changed when the familiar and rather sober teardrop motif is inverted, as at Mornington Crescent, London WC1 ABOVE. An influence upon this strange flower design could be the Greek anthemion. The Greek connection appears in the little palmette at the top.

The earliest houses in Great Ormonde Street, London WC1 date from the seventeenth century, but late eighteenth-century rectangular fanlights put in an appearance. At No. 3 BELOW is a rather flaccid oval somewhat resembling a meat dish, with garnishing in the form of eight stars. Four scrolls give it support from the corners.

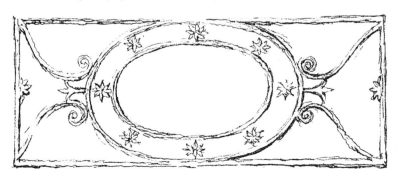

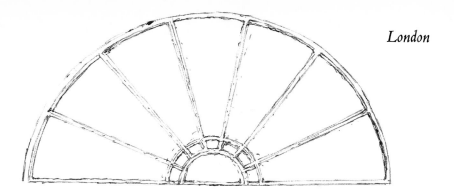

Charles Dickens lived at No. 48 Doughty Street, London WC1 ABOVE where the fanlight is rather plain. Nearby houses have fanlights and grilles of elliptical hoops. At No. 59 BELOW, five hoops fill the arch. At No. 58 another six hoops are added to the five ellipses to make an interlacing grille. At No. 60 the seven hoops are larger and rounder than those at No. 59, and consequently they must overlap.

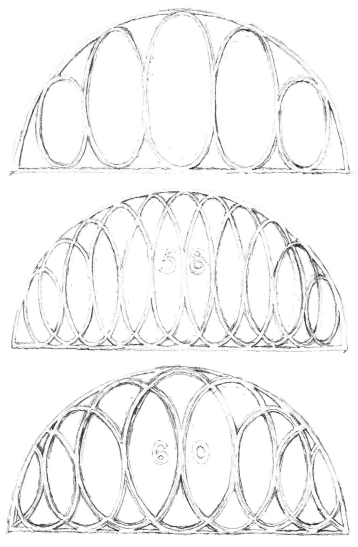

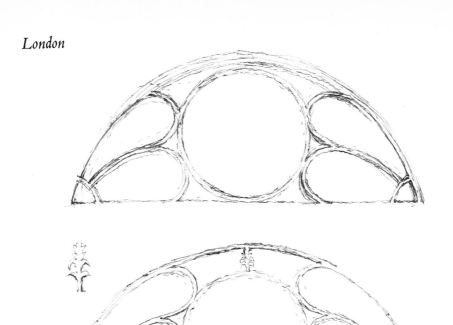

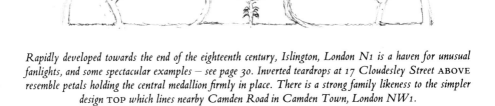

Rapidly developed towards the end of the eighteenth century, Islington, London N1 is a haven for unusual fanlights, and some spectacular examples — see page 30. Inverted teardrops at 17 Cloudesley Street ABOVE *resemble petals holding the central medallion firmly in place. There is a strong family likeness to the simpler design* TOP *which lines nearby Camden Road in Camden Town, London NW1.*

BELOW *At 108 Liverpool Road, London N1 there is not much harmony. The medallion tries to maintain a dignified position and shape in spite of the burden of two bulky teardrops on its shoulders and a pillow below, itself in discomfort from the insolent flower spike. Another flower spike contrives to allow space for another pair of tears to emerge.*

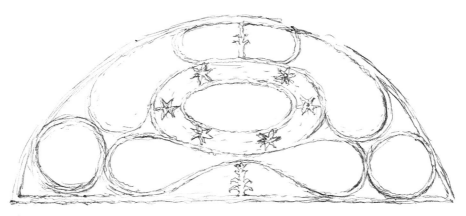

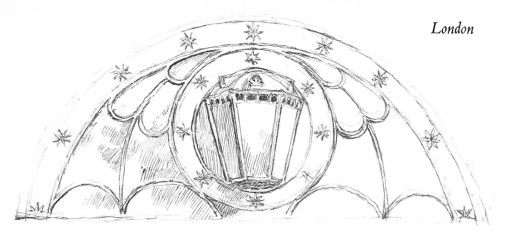

Just by the Angel, Islington, London N1, in Duncan Terrace, are gathered a number of marvellous fanlights. At No. 25 ABOVE there is around the edge a hemicycle of stars, then tears well up around a star-studded circle which, in turn, holds a lamp. The lamp, with a frieze of fleurs-de-lys, has three star-faced ventilators like tiny dormer windows. The tears, descending, arrive at the transom changed into batswings. The simpler, but elegant and unusual fanlight at No. 11 BELOW has a central medallion lightly supported by four scrolls.

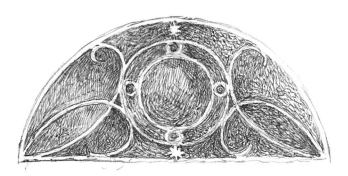

The three rings within the half circle at 3 and 12 Colebrooke Row, London N1 BELOW resemble a similar design at 34 Montagu Square (page 43). At Colebrook Row a two-way flower spike provides a centre line. It dates from 1768.

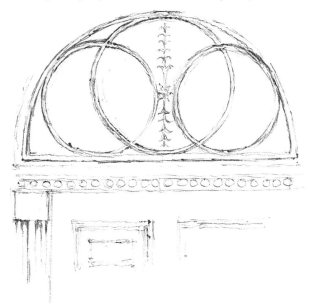

Among the larger houses on the Canonbury Estate is, at 5 Canonbury Place N1, a fanlight in the Adam style. Beneath an intermediate semicircle are rams' skulls with large horns that interlace, which they would not have been able to do had they been at the periphery. At the base of each spoke is a bony figure and we find each ray of the sun itself is a flower spike.

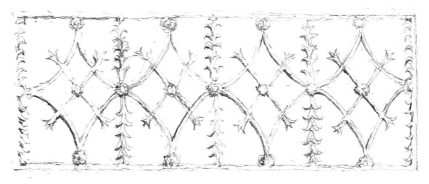

At the centre of the Lloyd Baker Estate between Islington and Clerkenwell is Granville Square, where all the houses in the upper half of the square have identical fanlights as ABOVE. *Giving the appearance of snowflakes, the lights are a most unusual and successful way of filling a long horizontal light. Four diamonds turn out to be composed of ogee curves disguised by the delicate ornamentation of floral devices and intersected by others to produce sixteen small diamonds. Although many of the details are now lost, there have been brave attempts at restoration and imitation.*

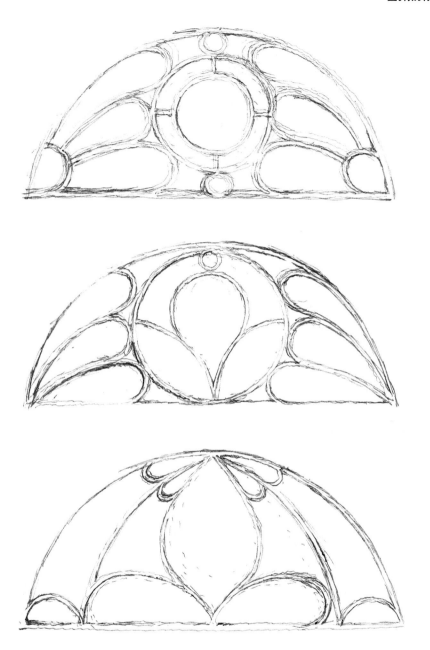

The fanlight at 39 Myddleton Square, Clerkenwell, London EC1 TOP *and at 20 Cloudesley Square, Islington N1* CENTRE *have medallions held in place by a trio of petals. At Cloudesley Square the medallion is decorated with a crocus. At 65 Gibson Square, Islington N1* ABOVE *the fanlight assumes several identities. Four teardrops emerge from the apex of the arch; a lemon-shaped centre is folded between batswings.*

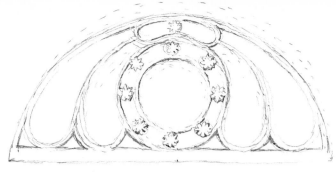

No. 9 River Street, EC1.

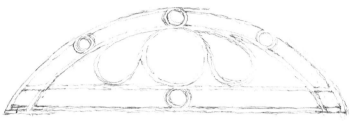

No. 13 Myddleton Square, EC1.

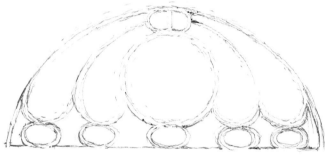

No. 12 River Street, EC1.

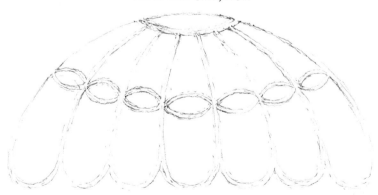

Inglebert Street, EC1.

The New River Estate was named after the scheme of Sir Hugh Myddleton in the seventeenth century to bring fresh water to London. In the eighteenth century on the surrounding open land houses were built. The four 'New River' fanlights illustrated here are all but one variations upon a theme — the medallion surrounded by batswing teardrops. The exception is at Inglebert Street, where the unusual umbrella design has a chain of eyes. A similar fanlight is over the inner lobby door.

The teardrop and batswing designs are beautifully illustrated by fanlights at 3 Wine Office Court, off Fleet Street, London EC4 ABOVE and 15 Wilkes Street, Spitalfields, London E1 TOP. Spitalfields contains some of London's most interesting old terraced houses, for the protection of which the Spitalfields Trust was formed. Some early houses had Bottomley fanlights inserted at the end of the eighteenth century, as at 23 Wilkes Street BELOW.

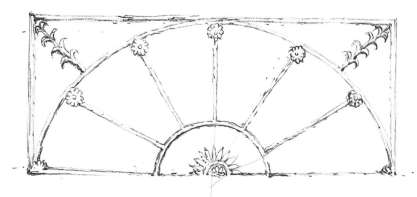

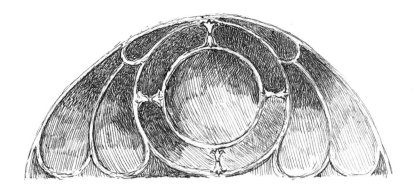

The Bishop of London's Estate was in Bayswater, London W2. In Albion Street, Nos. 11, 12, 13 and 14 ABOVE have fanlights identical except in their ornaments to No. 3 Wine Office Court (page 65). The fanlight at No. 34 Connaught Square W2 BELOW is Greek in inspiration both in the large fret around the perimeter and the large skeletal anthemion which the fret encompasses. Compare this embryo with the full flowering anthemion at Hume Street, Dublin (page 121). At No. 36 Connaught Square BOTTOM, paired spokes like columns and arches assume the representation of an arcade, the centre arch having a larger span to contain, possibly, the house number. Compare this with the lights at Nos. 1, 2 and 3 Regent Square WC1 and No. 11 Lloyd Street EC1, page 57.

This watercolour drawing shows us a Regency fanlight in its setting of slender Greek Doric fluted half-columns supporting an architrave and cornice combined, all within an arched recess. The fanlight itself, in tune with the sash windows of the period, has 'marginal bars' and provides a circle for the street number surviving here in the original characters of the period. It is No. 22 Hamilton Terrace, London NW8, part of the Eyre Estate.

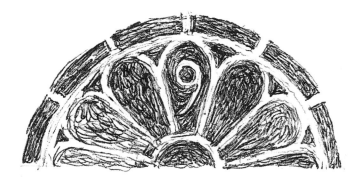

The estate of Henry S. Eyre in St John's Wood, London NW8 extended northwards from the Portman Estate as far as Belsize Road, eastwards to Primrose Hill and westwards to Edgware Road. The naming of Maida Vale after the British victory over Napoleon at Maida in Calabria in 1806 indicates the late date of development of this part of London, but a map exists from 1794 indicating the proposed building of pairs of semi-detached houses – an innovation which has certainly left its mark on this leafy suburb. The fanlights, all of late date, are of metal and generally conventional in design. On this and the facing page are five fanlights from Hamilton Terrace NW8. BELOW is No. 11, at the BOTTOM is No. 14.

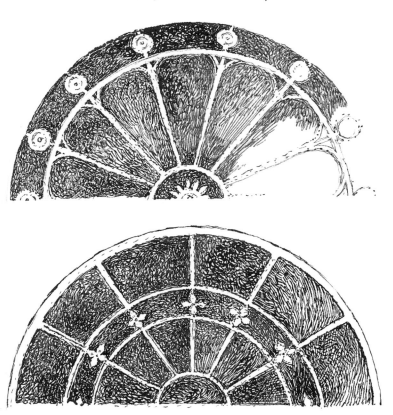

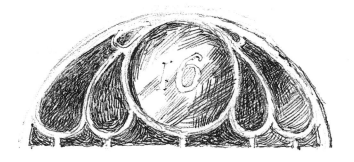

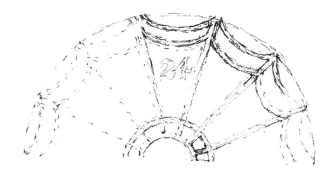

At No. 16 Hamilton Terrace, TOP *both the medallion containing the house number and the attendant teardrops fall short of the transom so each is supported by a small peg. In the light at No. 24,* ABOVE *we find the true fan again, with six spokes connected by a double row of festoons.*

At 33 St John's Wood Road, London NW8 is a pretty fanlight of pointed leaves within a border holding a ring at each leaf's end. A second half circle, interrupted by the leaves, gives them prominence.

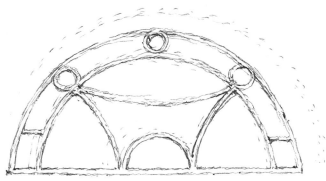

Over the small door of a small house, in No. 13 Abercorn Place,
London NW8, is the fanlight ABOVE. The figure within the margin
seems to suggest a game of 'cat's cradle'. Neighbouring fanlights at
16 and 17 Cunningham Place, London NW8 may be based on designs
from Underwood & Doyle's catalogue of 1813. At No. 16 BELOW
a teardrop design, it is possible that the large centre circle originally
held a lantern, and that some ornament has also disappeared from the
base, leaving the design bare, but striking. The beautiful diamond
inserted into the circle at No. 17 BOTTOM leaves the space too small
for either lantern or house number.

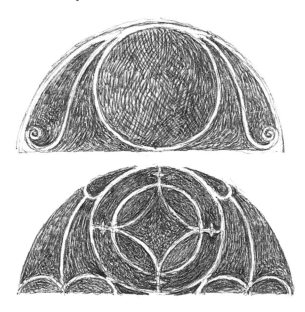

RIGHT *25 Church Row, Hampstead NW3. This watercolour drawing of a fanlight within its
setting of doorcase and door provides us with a lesson in architectural history. The beautiful surround of
the door, with its double-scroll brackets supporting a moulded and panelled door-hood, is one of several
in a row of early speculative houses built according to the Building Act of 1707. The design and workmanship
derives directly from the influence of Sir Christopher Wren and his chosen carver, Grinling Gibbons.
In some of the adjacent houses the original doors and fanlights exist (see pages 72–3) but here at No.
25 the fanlight and the door, replacements of half a century later, show the influence of the work of Robert
Adam. Even the railings are of the Adam period, replacing earlier Wren railings.*

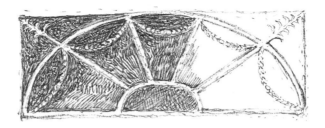

On either side of No. 25 Church Row, Hampstead NW3 illustrated on the previous page, are the late metal fanlight at No. 23 ABOVE and the early timber fanlight at No. 27 BELOW.

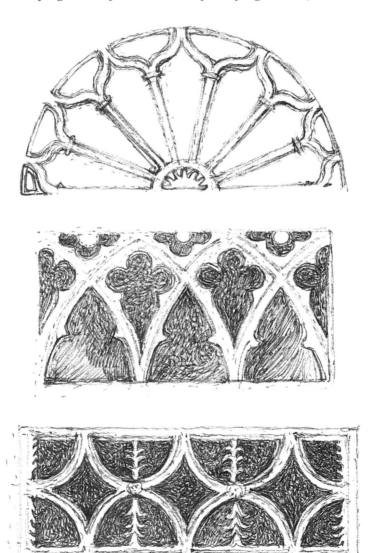

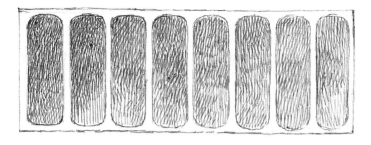

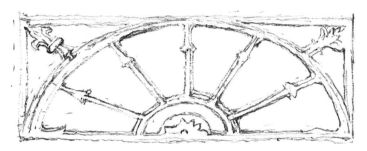

Church Row, Hampstead NW3. *The variety of fanlights in a single short street of houses built at the very beginning of the eighteenth century is shown on these pages. At No. 6* LOWER CENTRE, LEFT *is a pretty wood light in a rectangular frame carrying out the gothick idea, in earnest, for the bars have 'cusps'.* BOTTOM LEFT *No. 8 returns to the classic idiom with three diamonds en echelon, supported by flower spikes. At No. 9* TOP *is a light of the pattern usually found in houses of a later build. At No. 9a* ABOVE *an elliptical arch fills a wide rectangle; there are five and two half spokes enclosing a sun in the centre.*

BELOW *At No. 4 Mount Vernon, London NW3 is an elegant design in metal which recalls the more ornate version at No. 11 Duncan Terrace, Islington (see page 61).*

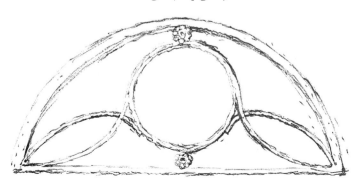

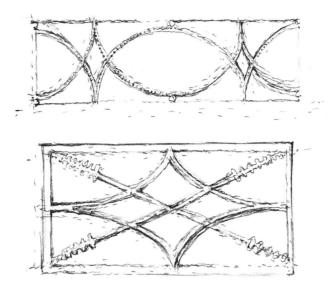

Five of the seven examples from Chelsea, London SW3, illustrated here and on the facing page are under arches, two in lintelled openings. The lintelled light at 22 Upper Cheyne Row TOP, where Leigh Hunt the literateur lived, is symmetrical about both centre lines to a simple pattern combining two half circles and four quarter circles. The light at 24 Upper Cheyne Row ABOVE follows a familiar pattern, which if not invented was certainly often used by Robert Adam. At 28 Cheyne Row BELOW the elegant design of the fanlight is created simply by a margin, two spokes and two loops. At adjacent No. 26 BOTTOM, the more conventional medallion design recalls No. 36 Trevor Square (see page 39), with two additional festoons.

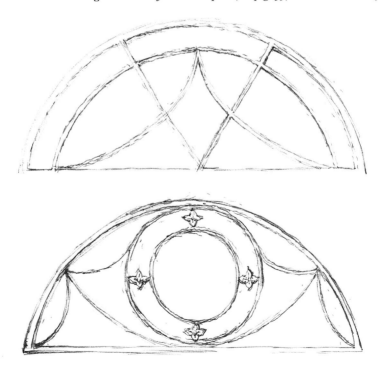

ABOVE *No. 91 Cheyne Walk, London SW3 has a very pretty flower pattern with petals and six arches in syncopated time with the petals. It could also be said to resemble a peacock's tail. At No. 37 Glebe Place* BELOW *the segmental shape of the opening contains two concentric semicircles, which tend to give the impression of improvisation, as though the design were an adaptation from another doorway.*

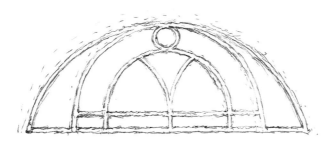

At No. 2 Carlyle Square BELOW, *where lived Sir Osbert Sitwell between 1919 and 1963, is the simple grille pattern found more usually in lintelled openings.*

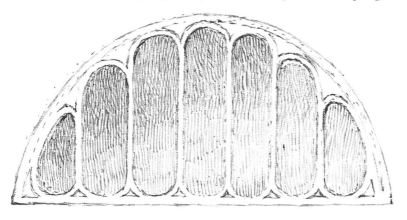

75

It was at the auction sale of the Brewery owned by his friends the Thrale family that Dr Johnson declared, 'We are not here to sell a parcel of boilers and vats but the potentiality of becoming rich beyond the dreams of avarice.' The purchasers were Courage. On Courage's property at Anchor Terrace, Southwark, London SE1, is the pretty fanlight ABOVE. Here the four spokes spring from lilies which surround a tiny sun whose rays are also florets. The spokes terminate in lilies beneath a double band containing rosettes. This leaves room for a beautiful arabesque around the periphery of the arch. In the ancient borough of Southwark, south of the Thames, are the traces of housing of varied status, and some working class terraces remain today. The fanlights at No. 8 St Thomas Street BELOW and 73–75 Stamford Street BOTTOM illustrate the not uncommon umbrella form. The adjacent houses in Stamford Street show, with the bulging shape of the central pane, the relationship to the batswing design. Both forms show the three-dimensional effect of a glazed apse which this design can create.

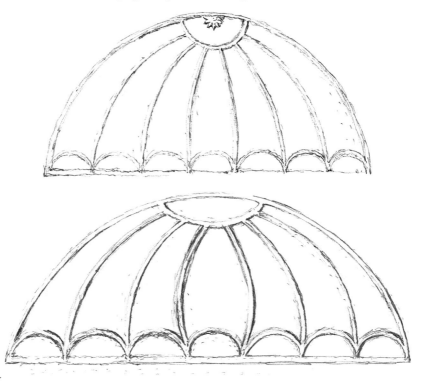

'Starting at Islington and going clockwise round London, there are strings of roadside terraces in Liverpool Road, Kingsland Road, Hackney Road, Mile End Road, and Commercial Road; and crossing the river, in the Old Kent Road, Walworth Road, Kennington Road, Kennington Lane and Lambeth Bridge Road.' John Summerson, in his admirable 'Georgian London', follows the development of housing at the end of the eighteenth century. In South London fanlights still line the roads that lead out from the centre of the city, though in many instances they are neglected.

ABOVE *is an architect's drawing for a substantial doorway in a terrace in Kennington Lane SE11. Though designs are rarely elaborate, in no part of London do fanlights deserve more attention and conservation than in the boroughs on the south of the Thames.*

The fanlight ABOVE at Etna House, 350 Kennington Road, London SE11, of the most refined type, shows us music and graphic design working to similar ideas. The six spokes beat the time while the three 'instruments' make their own time, the middle one breaking into syncopated time. The terrace of nine houses, Nos. 47 to 59 Harleyford Road SE11, has identical fanlights of the teardrop variety BELOW, with a central divided oval designed to allow the house number to occupy the centre.

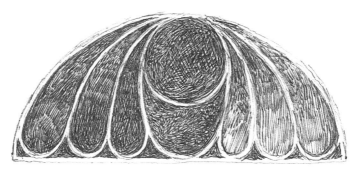

The most has been made of this rectangular light at 5 Pratt Walk, London SE11 BELOW to dispel the idea that the fan is confined. Cleverly the spokes of the fan extend to the confines of the rectangle, so that the double festoons disappear out of the picture.

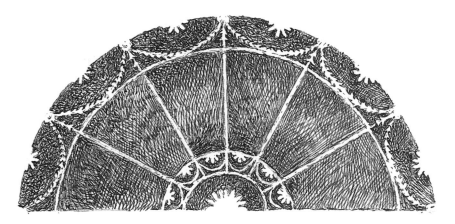

In south-east London, the areas richest in fanlights are Greenwich and Blackheath. At The Paragon, Blackheath, London SE3, designed by Michael Searles at the end of the eighteenth century, semi-detached pairs of houses are linked by colonnades. The semicircular fanlight illustrated here is quite orthodox. The five spokes are linked by loops at the perimeter and near the centre. At the centre of each loop is a half star or tiny sun. A full sun occupies the hub.

At 6 Montpelier Row, Blackheath, London SE3 the semicircular fanlight is filled with a mysterious figure in wood, from John Crunden's design of 1770.

Farnham in Surrey is one of many English country towns in which a characteristic style of fanlight is found, indicating a single maker. Of the eight fanlights from Castle Street illustrated in this book, the three ABOVE (Nos. 62, 70 and 71) are remarkable wooden lights from the eighteenth century made, no doubt, by a craftsman chairmaker, following patterns in books of the time.

By contrast, the rectangular fanlight at 4 Castle Street ABOVE *is a metal design based on a side light in the catalogue of Joseph Bottomley, 1795.*

At 14 Castle Street BELOW *is a narrow rectangle which we find in a taller version at 117 Hanover Street, Edinburgh (page 117), showing how this geometric design can be adapted to any proportion of rectangle without losing its identity.*

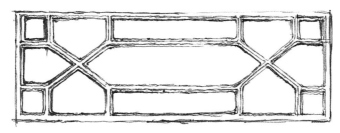

The fanlight at No. 61 Castle Street, Farnham BELOW *offers a good example of the device of grouping the spokes so that they assume architectural shape. See also designs in London at 27 Great James Street (page 37), 1, 2, 3 Regent Square (page 57), 11 Lloyd Street (page 57) and 36 Connaught Square (page 66).*

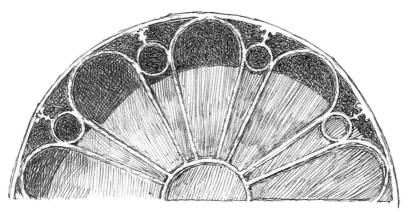

Also in Castle Street, Farnham are the two designs ABOVE, *each with a large sun at its centre.*

Bury St Edmunds in Suffolk is another town where fanlights show a local craftsman at work in timber (see pages 2, 84 and 85). The metal fanlights above and on the facing page adorn the entrances to Barclays and Lloyds Banks respectively. In both designs a pretty guilloche runs up to a star at the apex. At Lloyds Bank the transom is set low down, producing a stilted design. The downward extension of the fanlight has festoons, and allows a circular central panel which could include the house number.

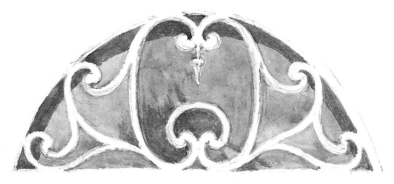

The beautiful rococo fanlights in wood at 8 St Anne's Place ABOVE *and 81a Guildhall Street, Bury St Edmunds,* RIGHT *are almost certainly by the same hand as that at 43 South Hill Park (see page 2). They share the 'chair-back' style with the wooden fanlights at Farnham (page 80) and Crunden's pattern book examples (page 15).*

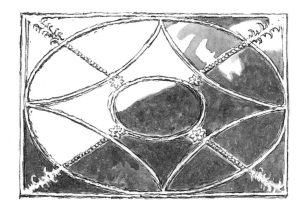

The metal fanlight ABOVE *at 6 Westgate Street, Bury St Edmunds is a modification of a Bottomley design, with a a central ellipse for the house number.* BELOW *at Chequer House, Chequer Square, an unusual metal fanlight has inverted teardrops like petals springing from the corners of the arch.*

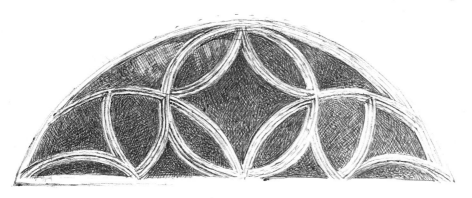

At Ansford near Castle Cary in Somerset two contrasting fanlights face each other on a bend in the road. The geometry of the fanlight ABOVE *is fascinating: using only two diameters, a lively pattern of diamond and circles is made which, nevertheless, recalls both batswing and Downing Street (page 39). Its partner* BELOW *is more delicate, with an elliptical arch.*

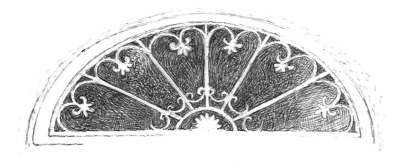

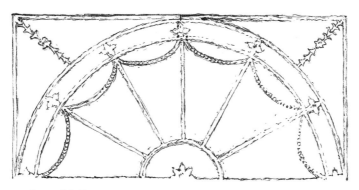

At 80 Guildhall Street, Bury St Edmunds, a fan design is housed within a rectangle. Spikes of flowers pointing two ways bisect the spandrels.

LEFT *In the beautiful stone town of Stamford in Lincolnshire is a stone version of the doorway carried out elsewhere in wood (see page 139). Here the pilasters and the frieze over are panelled. The fanlight has eight identical curved wooden bars making a diamond design which is repeated in the door itself.*

The gothick fanlight ABOVE at 37 North Street, Chichester, West Sussex, is of a type frequently encountered in wood in country towns. It sometimes contains more pointed arches, and is commonly adopted when the heads of adjacent sash windows are treated similarly.

This fanlight in North Street, Chichester ABOVE could be unique. It is a most unusual way of glazing a half circle, and very beautiful. The three balusters could have been made by a maker of gilt mirrors.

ABOVE *The Fernleigh Centre, Chichester.*

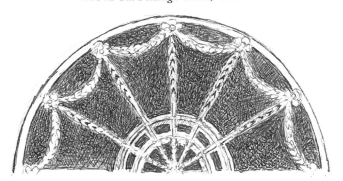

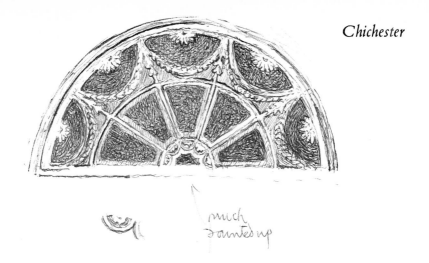

The designs on this page and opposite are all from Chichester, West Sussex. The radial designs LEFT BELOW and ABOVE from North Street include some interesting detailing in the form of corn husks and garlands. At 61 North Street BELOW are nine spokes in an elliptical arch. The arrival of these nine spokes at the centre is strangely interrupted by the oval which squats awkwardly over the low sunrise. At 68 North Street BOTTOM, in a low elliptical arch, the classical fan of five spokes and their festoons is crossed in a curiously nonchalant way by an ogee gothick arch.

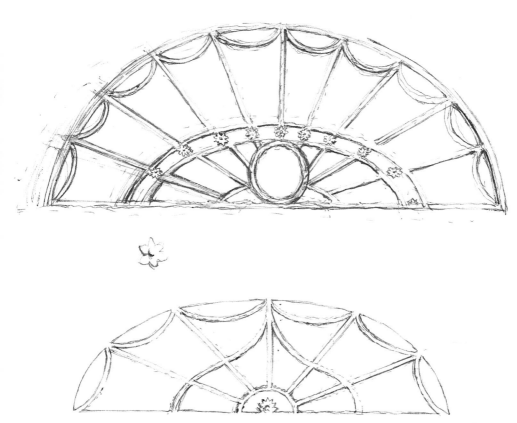

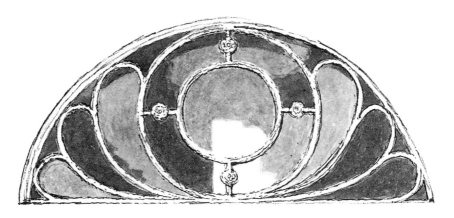

The fanlights in Cheltenham, Gloucestershire, are mainly from the nineteenth century, as their rather rigid forms indicate. ABOVE *No. 5 St Georges Terrace and* TOP RIGHT *90 Bath Road show elegant traditional designs with space for house numbers in the centre circles. A house number could fit in the centre of the rectangular design* BELOW *at 4 Clarence Square, but not at 4 Grafton Road* BOTTOM. *Is it possible that here the cross in the central oval was inserted when the glazier had not a large enough pane of glass? The marginal panes in these Regency lights often contained coloured glass.*

At Lauriston House, Montpellier, Cheltenham ABOVE CENTRE, *a vertical grille pattern is typical of the Regency or early Victorian terrace house. At Oriel lodge, Oriel Road, Cheltenham* ABOVE, *gothick window tracery patterns fill this gothick arch, but the work is essentially that of the metal-craftsman, not of the stonemason.*

Bath

The remarkable expansion of the City of Bath beyond its medieval confines was due largely to the activities of three men, Richard 'Beau' Nash (1674-1762), Ralph Allen (1694-1764) and the architect John Wood (1704-54). Nash, who had been at Jesus College Oxford, had obtained an army commission and had studied law at the Temple, succeeded Captain Webster as Master of Ceremonies at Bath in 1705. Nash found Bath dirty, dangerous and extortionate and its reputation as a 'watering-place' low. Nash stopped the wearing of swords and boots in 'drawing rooms', controlled the conditions and the charges of lodgings and brought Bath to a standard where investment in new buildings became attractive.

Once order was established, the first requirement for the expansion was land. A surgeon, John Gay, owned the fields north-west of the city. Next an architect was required. Born in Bath but working in London and Yorkshire, John Wood had the advantage of experience over the local builders. He showed builders how to prepare the stone on the 'banker'—that is, prepare it for its selected place on the building. Easily worked, the Bath stone had been laid with little regard for its final shape. Wood had it prepared on the 'banker', giving a fine control of detail. Finally came the financier, who also owned the quarries, which were actually mines. He was Ralph Allen, who earned the gratuitous title 'Man of Bath'. And so the three, Gay, Allen and Wood, conceived and realised the most dignified set of buildings seen in England before or since, in particular Gay Street, Queen Square and the Circus. John Wood junior followed from 1767 onwards, and built the Royal Crescent (from 1789) and Pulteney Street.

All these, in the Palladian style, provided a perfect setting for the fanlight, whether in a plain arched doorway or under a pediment or entablature, or between a pair of columns or pilasters.

Successful at these ventures, Ralph Allen built Prior Park to advertise his stone, and then improved navigation on the River Avon so that he could send his stone to Bristol. He persuaded James Gibbs in London to use it on St Bartholomew's Hospital and Lord Burlington to use it on Westminster School Dormitory.

The illustrations which follow show some of the designs in Bath today, a city which in spite of savage demolition in recent decades is now conscious of the elegance of its Georgian buildings both grand and humble.

LEFT *No. 3 Cavendish Place, Bath.*

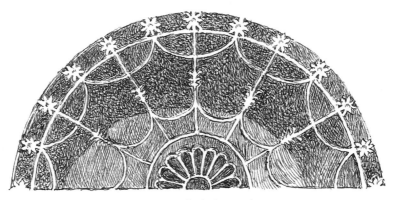

No. 7 Portland Place, Bath.

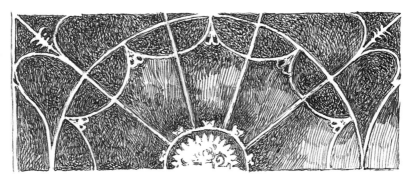

No. 15 Somerset Place, Bath.

No. 8 George Street, Bath.

ABOVE *Delicate fanlights in Bath of the Eldorado type, c.1800.* RIGHT *An Eldorado fanlight at 7 Lansdowne Crescent, Bath, deeply recessed within its beautiful bevelled ashlar wall.*

ABOVE *No. 8 Russel Street, Bath. A simple stone surround and archivolt contain a fanlight of seven petals.* RIGHT *No. 9 Gay Street, Bath. Most of the work in Bath, under the architectural discipline imposed by the Woods, father and son, maintained a highly orthodox style. Here the doorway is of the correct Ionic Order with its proper modillioned cornice. But is the fanlight intended for a flower design, or is it a teardrop design put in upside-down? The building was restored in 1977. Would such a daring reversal have been made at such a time?*

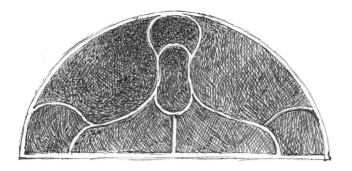

ABOVE *A curiosity in Bathwick Street, Bath, important to preserve if only for that reason.* BELOW *A rectangular light in the same street, based on a design by Underwood & Doyle. The related design* BOTTOM *at Old Market House, Maltravers Street, Arundel, West Sussex, comes straight from the Underwood & Doyle catalogue of 1813.*

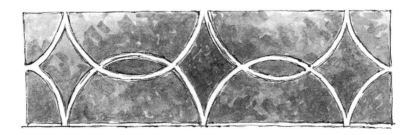

LEFT *No. 5 Hay Hill, Bath. It would appear that the unusual gas lantern inserted in this fanlight was intended from the start. How else would the spokes of the fanlight have been so arranged? The fluted pilasters of the doorcase support a pediment pierced by the arch containing the fanlight, a practice which extended throughout Britain during the eighteenth century.*

No. 22 Royal York Crescent, Bristol.

Bristol

How did the merchants and sailors of Bristol contend with the fifty-foot tide in the River Avon? They built their ships with flat bottoms—ship-shape and 'Bristol fashion'—and 'Bristol fashion' was the way the Bristolians conducted their affairs. 'Bristol fashion' was how they set up the 'Nails' in the tollbooth for paying 'on the nail'; 'Bristol fashion' how they established the powerful Company of the Merchant Adventurers and 'Bristol fashion' how their speculators, builders and architects tackled their cliffs and hills when level building land became scarce.

Bristol fashion, they eventually by-passed the River Avon by the 'New-Cut' and dredged out the Floating Harbour, thereby freeing their sailors from the awful tides. Before that Bristol had a constant struggle to provide enough anchorage for the quays from which John Cabot and his sons had set sail to discover a new route to Asia, and discovered Greenland and Newfoundland instead.

Spared a great conflagration like London's, the Elizabethan and Jacobean houses of Bristol survived well into the nineteenth century. Hundreds of photographs record them before most were replaced by the massive Byzantine and Venetian-styled warehouses and counting houses of the Bristol merchants.

Land for house-building outside the city became scarce after King Street, Prince Street and Queen Square on the 'Marsh' had been built and, across the Frome, Orchard Street had occupied the grounds of Queen Elizabeth's Hospital. On heights north of the Frome some level land lay. Here were built Brunswick Square, St James's Square, Portland Square, Kingsdown Parade and, round its ilex tree in a circular lawn, Fremantle Square.

Downstream along the Avon, where hot springs had been discovered, alleged to possess medicinal properties, were built Dowry Square, Albemarle Row and the Colonnade for visitors to the wells. Immediately beyond, the St Vincent's Rocks had been noticed already by the diarist John Evelyn, and the dramatic effect of the

River Avon at the foot of this tremendous cliff appealed to lovers of the picturesque. In the next century, poets and the sons of the gentry who, with their tutors, began to do the Grand Tour, may have been reminded here of their first sight of Genoa or Naples as they approached those Italian ports from the sea. Here the works of man had already added to those of nature. By the end of the eighteenth century the works of man had begun to appear upon the dizzy heights of Clifton.

In the earlier terraces and squares of the eighteenth century it was the new squares and streets of London that had guided the builders. In Bristol red facing bricks were laid over their random stone walling. At first the window arches were like those of London and Dublin, of gauged brick. Soon they were to be of stone cut into 'voussoirs', each one higher than the last, each slightly forward, until the keystone is reached. To complement this pretty device, on the face of the terrace at each party wall from base to coping, a vertical pattern of long and short stones was laid. As in London and Dublin, further embellishment of the house fronts was left to the front doors, iron railings, lamp-holders and, of course, their fanlights.

When stone came to be used more freely, whole house fronts were faced in Bath Stone, which became more available when Ralph Allen improved the channel of the Avon for bringing stone from the quarries at Coombe Down.

Although pattern books were available from London, those by James Gibbs and Isaac Ware being the most used, Bristol's own architects, chiefly the Paty family, not only designed houses and terraces but made and sold stone door cases, window surrounds and fireplaces and, in fact, practised as did the Adams in Edinburgh. In fact William Paty the son had studied at the Royal Academy Schools at Somerset House, London.

The assault upon the Clifton heights began when available flat land had become scarce. In spite of financial distress brought about by the war with France, the indomitable spirit of the Bristol speculators eventually allowed the crescents and terraces of Clifton to be finished. Charles Dickens put it thus: '... away he walked, up one street and down another—we were going to say up one hill and down another only its all uphill at Clifton.' (*Pickwick Papers*, Chapter 24)

Messrs Gomme, Jenner & Little put it well: 'A plan of Clifton gives no indication of the formidable hills which had to be encountered ... In Clifton the topography is what counts most; the architectural and landscape setting of the terrace is all important, the details secondary. To the stranger a street plan would suggest that Windsor Terrace is only a few yards from Hotwells Road and the river, but Windsor Terrace ends in a cliff a hundred feet above. Immediately north-east the Paragon is seventy-five feet higher again and Royal York Crescent is twenty feet above the Paragon, while Cornwallis Crescent is the same distance below.' (*Bristol, an Architectural History*)

What the architects and builders of Clifton may have lacked in detail they gave full measure in variety. They built Royal York Crescent to a very gentle curve and put it upon a terrace supported by great arches, as did the brothers Adam at their Adelphi on the Thames (demolished), while they built Cornwallis Crescent also upon arches with its even gentler curve facing its garden. They faced the convex curve of the Paragon towards the view and the sun, the concave side to the road, to which they added little round porches in a style described today as 'Mannerist'. In front of Windsor Terrace they put a great paved square approached through splendid cast⁄iron gate piers.

Clifton, its scenic attractions thus enhanced by man's endeavours, was to receive a final crown also from the works of man—the Suspension Bridge.

Although Clifton continued to grow over the more level high ground it was not as a spa resort. Its houses here were built for permanent residents, although in appearance the houses began to resemble those of Bath. For at the resumption of building after the hiatus caused by the French wars a change to a more severe Imperial Roman style meant that the front door was not the important feature it had been; it stepped down to allow the lofty colonnade to take the stage. The fanlight consequently became a mere rectangle filled by a simple wood fanlight of geometric design.

These few remarks can do no more than sketch the setting in Bristol of our principal study, the fanlights of the last quarter of the eighteenth century and the first quarter of the nineteenth. This Bristol and Clifton scene, a subject of such interest and complication, has been presented superbly by Walter Ison, FSA, in *The Georgian Buildings of Bristol*. This was followed in 1979 by Andor Gomme, Michael Jenner and Brian Little in *Bristol, an Architectural History*. In 1958 Sir Nikolaus Pevsner warned us: 'Architects and promoters have to think of some way to keep Clifton Clifton. I emphatically do not mean that as an appeal for neo⁄Georgian and new⁄Regency.' (*The Buildings of England: North Somerset and Bristol*)

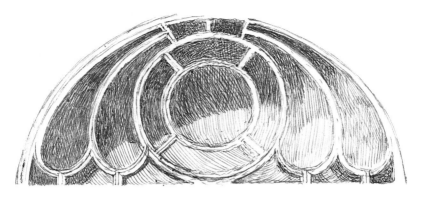

No. 6 Harley Place, Clifton, Bristol.

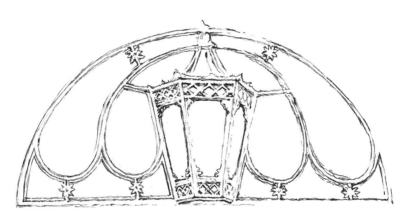

Most of the fanlights in Bristol are in Georgian Clifton. The classic teardrop design at 6 Harley Place TOP *encloses a medallion for the house number. At No. 4 Royal York Crescent* ABOVE *the central area is occupied by a fine lantern. In some instances, as here, it is difficult to tell if the lantern is contemporary or a later insert. The teardrop design* BELOW *with its elliptical central frame is from No. 7 Marine Square, Brighton, East Sussex.*

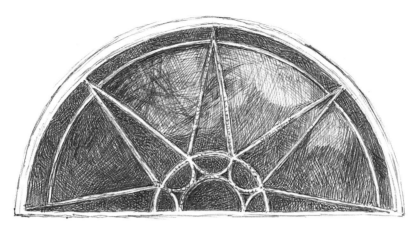

At No. 32 Caledonian Place, Clifton ABOVE *is a fan with a harlequin touch. The radials are paired to form points, while the loops at the centre complete the figure. The way the margin allows the points to pierce it, thereby supplying its support, is a touch of genius.*

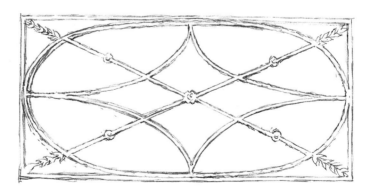

At No. 13 Sion Hill, Clifton ABOVE *is a version of a Bottomley design of 1795. This can be adapted to fit a long rectangle, as here, but in so doing the ellipse becomes rather ungainly. The design is seen without its ellipse in Chelsea (page 74) and, further modified, in Bury St Edmunds (page 85).*

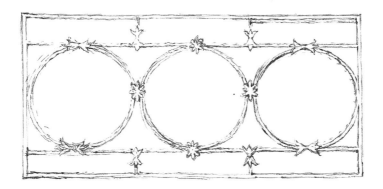

The three rectangular lights from Clifton, Bristol ABOVE *are symmetrical about two bisectors. The lantern — probably a late insertion — at Harley Place* TOP *hides a 'meat dish' medallion. To accommodate the three circles in the light at Sion Hill* CENTRE *a margin with floral ornaments has been added top and bottom. In the ingenious design at No. 31 Caledonian Place* ABOVE *the margins bend around the circles like a toy train track.*

Three conventional 'peacock's tail' metal fanlights from Bristol: ABOVE *and* BELOW
from Great George Street, Brandon Hill, and BOTTOM *No. 3 Harley Place, Clifton,
where the fan is enlivened with circles in the outer margin.*

RIGHT *No. 46 St Michael's Hill, Bristol. The grandness of this Bath stone porch, probably from the
yard of the Paty family, makes the front door itself look modest. The orthodox metal fanlight returns
the entrance way to domestic elegance.*

ABOVE *No. 23 Cornwallis Crescent, Clifton, Bristol. A continuous stone archivolt surrounds both door and fanlight. The fanlight is of the teardrop variety. Was the pretty lantern added?* RIGHT *No. 27 Rodney Street, Liverpool. This fanlight surmounts a door set between a pair of columns of the Greek Revival, thinned down to the proportions appropriate to wood. Over-painting has robbed the seven-petalled fanlight of its original delicacy.*

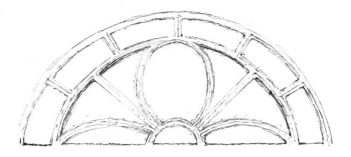

There is a family likeness between the Georgian doorways of Liverpool, illustrated here, and Dublin. In the brick terraces, Adam-style fanlights are often recessed deep within the arch above heavy and ornate Greek entablature and paired columns. The doorway LEFT is 20 Falkner Street, and on the previous page is from Rodney Street, one of the finest Georgian streets in the country, built between 1780 and 1840. Most houses reflect the prestigious lifestyle of Liverpool merchants, but not all the houses in Rodney Street have such ornate doorways. Some follow the 'umbrella' design popular after 1800, and at Nos. 66 and 68 ABOVE is a simple petal form, with a margin containing unornamented bars. In the rectangular fanlight BELOW the design from two square figures is improved by the omission of the central bar.

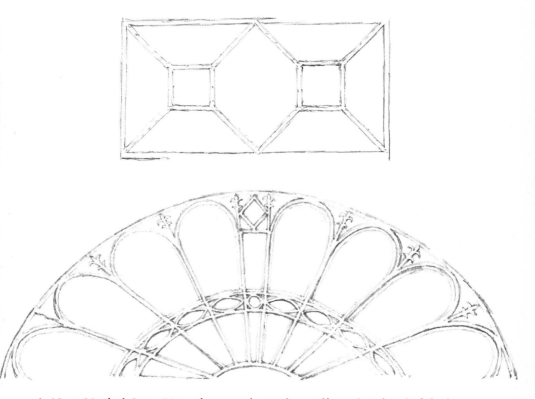

At No. 2 Maryland Street, Liverpool ABOVE the intruding entablature (not shown) of the doorway into the semicircle of the arch forces the Adam-style fanlight into a segmental form. Two spokes come close together in the centre, and the whole, now heavily overpainted, is less than elegant.

ABOVE *Also in Rodney Street, Liverpool, at No. 84 and elsewhere is a grand fanlight with eight spokes, very elegant, without ornament. Linking the spokes are scrolls forming arches more Persian than gothick, with a tiny top-knot at the apex of each.*

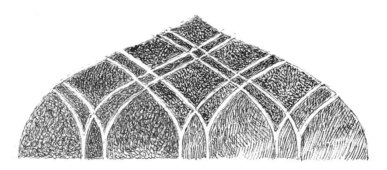

In 1837 a terrace of small houses was built in Donegall Pass, then on the outskirts of the city of Belfast, Northern Ireland, where not only the doorway but the windows too sported gothick fenestration under four-centred arches.

No. 61 North Castle Street, Edinburgh.

Edinburgh New Town

Until the second half of the eighteenth century, Edinburgh was still a small, crowded, medieval town, confined between walls, as were most towns in Europe, but restricted by its situation to a narrow rocky ridge, with one main street leading up to the castle. On each side steep and narrow 'wynds' descended to a valley, that on the north containing North Loch. In spite of some brave efforts to expand the Old Town, as it came to be called, the demand for better homes and for the public buildings necessary for a capital city could not be met without expansion. All those obliged to live in Edinburgh had to inhabit tall, narrow, often rickety buildings containing 'flats'—the term 'flat', as in America, applied to a whole floor in a block, each to a family.

Some extensions had been made at the lower end of the ridge but no definite move was made by the Provost and Town Council until prompted by a pamphlet: *Proposals for carrying on certain Public Works in the City of Edinburgh.* This pamphlet, written by Sir Gilbert Elliot, owed much to George Drummond, a remarkable man who became Lord Provost in 1725 and held office five times in all. Drummond's abiding interest was the founding of the Royal Infirmary. He had fought at Preston Pans against the Jacobites and now, in 1752, aged sixty-five, he entered whole-heartedly in support of the *Proposals*. To a contemporary, standing with Drummond at a window in the Old Town and looking across the fields which contained the North Loch, Drummond said: 'Look at these fields; you are a young man and will probably live, though I will not, to see all these fields covered with houses, forming a splendid and magnificent city. To the accomplishment of this nothing is necessary other than draining the North Loch, and providing a proper access from the Old Town. I have never lost sight of this object since the year 1725 when I was first elected Provost.'

113

This conversation took place in 1768. Sixteen years before, an accident had occurred in the Old Town endorsing, if endorsement were needed, the urgency of expansion. The side wall of a six-storey house, containing at least as many families, collapsed. This led to a survey of other houses in danger of falling and several were pulled down, leaving gaps.

The decision of the Town Council to extend the 'Royalty' (town boundary) of Edinburgh was already confirmed sufficiently for construction of the North Bridge to be started in 1763, and in 1766 the Council called for plans for the 'New Town'. Of the six plans received that by James Craig was accepted. Craig's plan owes its success to its simplicity and to its good proportions. The plan proposed three streets running the length of the New Town, the centre one ending at each end in a square, the outer streets to be built upon *one side only* forming promenades, one providing views of the Old Town, the other a view of the country.

Between the squares were to be cross streets, dividing the site into eight blocks of the ideal 'golden mean' proportions of the seventeenth century. Down the centre of each block were to be lines of coach houses and stables with rooms for coachmen and ostlers. No building regulations were issued by the Town Council, but the ground landlords provided the small *feuars* (the nearest English equivalent is 'lease-holders') with regulations controlling the height and construction of the houses, and specified the quarries for the supply of grey sandstone. As in London, the leases or 'feus' were taken up either by the builders, the architects or the intending residents. Seven quarries were named, the most used being Craigleith.

Two changes were made to Craig's plan. First, St Andrew's church had to be put in the centre of the George Street houses instead of occupying the focal point in St Andrew's Square, for this site had been taken in 1767 by Sir Laurence Dundas for a splendid house, now the Royal Bank of Scotland, designed by Sir William Chambers, who also designed 35 St Andrew's Square. A second change to

The seven spokes of the light at 17 Moray Place, Edinburgh are connected at the intermediate ring by round arches and at the outer ring by ogee arches with flower spikes between.

The exceptional history of the planning and building of Edinburgh's New Town and the consistency of its stone buildings, some by Robert Adam, have established for it a place in the iconography of the fanlight. The maintenance of the New Town is assisted by expert guidance contained in 'A Maintenance Manual for Edinburgh New Town' (see Bibliography), in which fanlights have been made a special study. This magnificent fanlight at 25 Melville Street is typical Edinburgh. We find a familiar motif reduced to modest size by the twelve rays or petals in the outer ring, while in the centre is a delightful device which makes fun of the surrounding teardrops.

Craig's plan was made when Robert Adam provided a new plan for St George's Square, calling it Charlotte Square. This involved the first occasion in the New Town when, as intended by Wood at Queen Square, Bath, the façades on each side of the square were designed as a complete 'composition', as if each side was the façade of a palace.

Although wars and rumours of war and other vicissitudes did not favour continual or consistent construction of houses, in the next century the New Town expanded beyond the limits of Craig's long rectangle. After 1800 expansion took place on land beyond the boundaries of the town's 'Royalty'. The owners were Heriot's Hospital, the Earl of Moray, Sir Francis Walker and the painter Henry Raeburn. Here Royal Circus and Drummond Place, connected by Great King Street, were designed by Reid and Sibbald. The estate of Henry Raeburn received a large increase upon his marriage and this enlarged estate was built upon. Land, now Ann Street and India Place, belonging to the Earl of Moray, was built upon under the careful eye of the earl, who employed James Gillespie Graham to design Moray Place (1824-27). Anxious to prevent the variations that had shown already in the New Town, the earl issued very exacting requirements for his estate.

Built between 1775 and 1790, St James's Square to the east of the New Town was also by James Craig. It started well, with palace fronts, plain but dignified. Becoming unfashionable and consequently badly used, it has since been demolished. Any visitor to Edinburgh today, however, will see how well kept are the buildings in and beyond the New Town, and how a special character attaches to Edinburgh fanlights, as the drawings which follow show.

ABOVE *No. 8 Moray Place, Edinburgh. Being under a large arch, it is fortunate that the designer limited his chosen subject, the batswing, to a reasonable size. To achieve this he has provided at the perimeter an extra large chain of eight circles interspersed with flower sprigs, and at the centre a generous medallion with a margin of stars containing the large house number. And so the modest batswing does not either scare or overwhelm the visitor.*

Many Edinburgh fanlights are relatively tall rectangles. The semicircle holding the seven spokes at 4 Melville Street TOP RIGHT *does not quite fill the rectangle and so there is an extension above the transom marked off like five bricks. Elongated lozenges fill each spandrel like a pair of ears. The design* BOTTOM RIGHT *at 117 Hanover Street is a late one adapted to a tall frame (see page 81). At No. 35 London Street* CENTRE RIGHT *the design is confined by margins all round — a late pattern.*

At No. 38 India Street, Edinburgh ABOVE *we have the teardrop confined to an upper storey raised upon an arcaded undercroft and with little headroom.*

No. 4 Melville Street, Edinburgh.

No. 35 London Street, Edinburgh.

No. 117 Hanover Street, Edinburgh.

No. 61 Dundas Street, Edinburgh.

Rectangular designs in Edinburgh. The intricate designs BELOW *at No. 53 Albany Street and* TOP RIGHT *at 15 Dundas Street may be intended as grilles.* CENTRE AND BOTTOM RIGHT *The umbrella starts to unfurl (see page 120).*

No. 53 Albany Street, Edinburgh.

15 Dundas Street, Edinburgh.

25 Ann Street, Edinburgh.

31 Ann Street, Edinburgh.

Typical of the early nineteenth century are the 'umbrella' designs shown here from 13 Great King Street ABOVE *and 1 Northumberland Place* TOP, *Edinburgh, where the effect is quite three-dimensional. At 43 Albany Street* BELOW *the umbrella is raised on a base with ogee arches between the spokes, and more curves in the spandrels.*

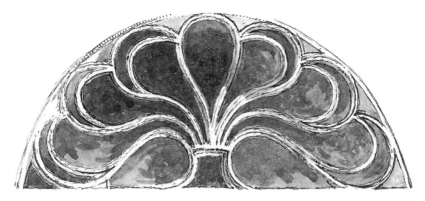

A Greek anthemion to enormous scale at Hume Street, Dublin.

Dublin

Modern Dublin can be said to date from 27 July, 1662, when the Protestant Duke of Ormonde returned to Dublin as Viceroy after an exile of thirteen years serving Louis XIV of France. He was fifty-two and Dublin was the chief garrison of the English Pale, one-sixth of the size of medieval London. Dublin then stood south of the Liffey.

The first of Dublin's great undertakings under Ormonde was the establishment of Phoenix Park, still containing 1750 acres and one of the finest parks in the world. In 1662 St Stephen's Green, College Green and Oxmantown Green, each comparable in size to London's Lincoln's Inn Fields, were added as a green belt.

In the eighteenth century a simple and fundamental device enabled Dublin to steal a march over Bristol and London in the matter of town planning. This was the Wide Streets Act of 1757, ratified nine times afterwards and controlled by the Wide Streets Commission. By this excellent Act the Commissioners were empowered to purchase houses and their sites compulsorily. The first street constructed under the Act was opened in 1762 and named Parliament Street. It was fifty-eight feet wide. 'These enactments, well in advance of their time, show a high degree of enlightened planning. They left a Dublin the breadth of whose streets still astonished the stranger.' (Maurice Craig)

Later streets were wider: Sackville (now Lower O'Connell) Street 154 feet wide, Westmoreland Street 96 feet, Upper Merrion Street 102 feet, Baggot Street 100 feet, Gardiner Street 85 feet wide, and Dominick Street 74 feet. These were earlier than the Prince Regent's Regent Street, London, and earlier still than the London County Council's Kingsway.

But there were no Irish Building Acts. Control over the standards of planning and of building was exercised through the building leases which specified thickness of walls and kept frontages to uniform height. The Act requiring the wood crowning cornice to be removed as in London was never enacted: the wood

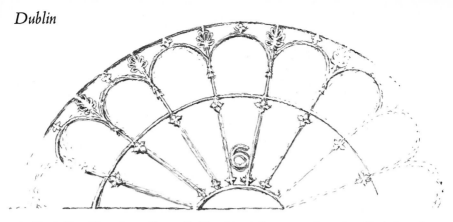

At No. 6 Fitzwilliam Street Upper, Dublin, eight shafts support nine arches. Perched on the crown of each arch like a cross is a four-petalled flower. At the head of the shaft and between the arches is a palmette.

box-frames of the windows were required by a provision of the lease to be set back, whereas in London it was, of course, the law.

The grey stock bricks of the walls were burnt locally, but 'not within two miles of street lamps'. Red facing bricks, so characteristic of Dublin, came from Bridg-water, Somerset.

The earliest houses to line Dublin's new wide streets were large by comparison with London's: the smallest Dublin houses would have been classed as 'first rate'. After about 1780 plans became more standardised.

The passage of time, and some of its first and wealthiest inhabitants, brought change. While the Gardiners were busy on the north-east of Dublin, the Fitzwill-iams began on the south-east and, like Luke Gardiner, Earl Fitzwilliam started with a short wide street—Upper Merrion Street—and continued with the three sides of Merrion Square (for Leinster Lawn forms one side).

The sixth Lord Fitzwilliam began about 1750 an orderly scheme of develop-ment which went on coherently for at least a hundred years, making what is now the best quarter in Dublin. The Fitzwilliam Estate passed to the Earls of Pembroke, who still administer it. Other Dublin estates in this category are the Molesworth and the Beresford-Tyrone. However, the largest landlords in Dublin were not the great earls but the City Corporation itself.

The initial scale which the wider streets of Dublin have given to the street scene, supported by the more generous scale of the town houses in the best streets, has given 'Dublin Georgian' a special meaning. The beautiful doorcases, still embellished by their surviving fanlights, recall those doorways perfectly preserved in Colonial and Federal houses of America. There is a strong link in design and craftsmanship between the 'double-fronted' houses with generous hallways lit by fanlights and side lights, which occur more frequently in Ireland and America than in England.

Noticeable in some Irish fanlights, occurring also in America, is the outer ring, over the side lights, of an opaque hemicycle decorated with moulded plaster fes-toons in the Adam or Pompeian style (see page 127).

A typical ornate Dublin fanlight with side lights and engaged columns at No. 57 Merrion Square North.

BELOW *No. 25 Fitzwilliam Square, Dublin. In this fanlight the eight spokes are linked midway by half-round arches, under a double ring containing seventeen tiny circles. Each spoke then becomes the centre of a strange device, less gothick, more Persian. At No. 47 Leeson Square, Dublin* BOTTOM *is a gothick fantasia with a Persian flavour. The eight spokes continue from hub to circumference, linked by ogee quatrefoils. Between these and the perimeter are trefoils, their delicate cusps forming the shape of the petals of a violet.*

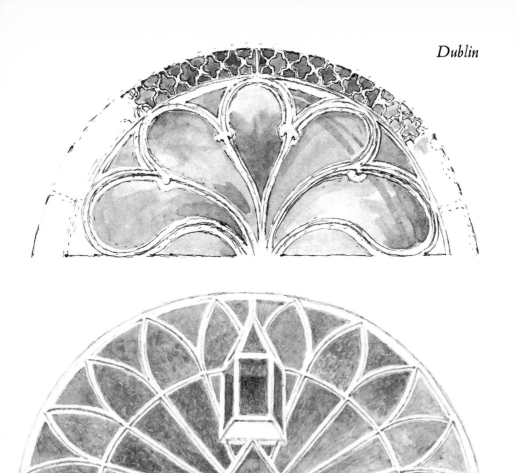

At Fitzwilliam Square East TOP *is a beautiful flower. Around the periphery is a chain of minute quatrefoils.* ABOVE *is a truly gothick Dublin design, with its tall lantern raised high among the petals by the diamond at its hub. Compare with the design on page 128.*

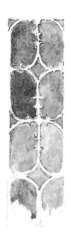

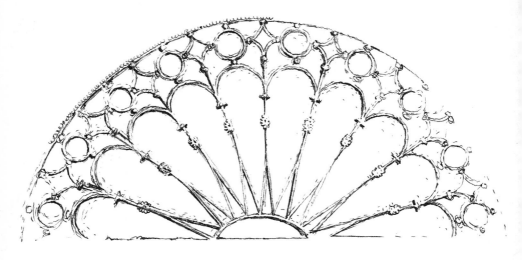

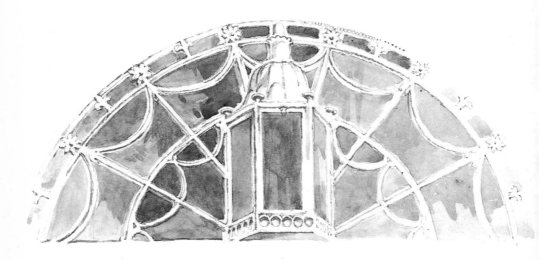

At Merrion Square Upper TOP *we find several motifs in a delicate design. The sun's rays turn out to be columns supporting arches, with a chain of diamonds and circles around the perimeter. At Ely Place, Dublin* ABOVE *an Adam design with syncopated festoons has had an elegant lantern added, with its own lantern crowning an ogee dome.*

At No. 37 Merrion Square, Dublin RIGHT *blind plasterwork with festoons creates a semicircle the width of the doorway and its side lights, but the impression it gives is of a Palladian or Venetian window. Substitution of plaster for glass became necessary when the floor above came below the arch.*

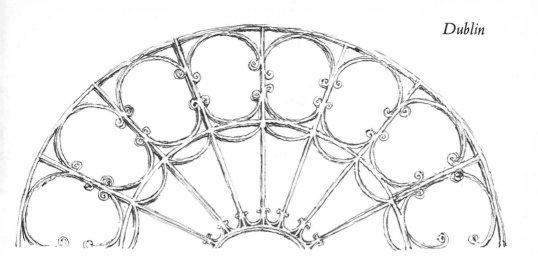

At Fitzwilliam Square South TOP are, on the perimeter of the fanlight, eight scrolls with partners in an inverted position, forming together a chain of oval shapes, with more scrolls around the hub. The finely wrought and beautiful fanlight at No. 9 Hume Street, Dublin ABOVE was evidently the work of a sensitive craftsman. Outside the glorious corona comes a chain with a ribbon winding in and out within a hemi-cycle. Then a chain of gothick figures, like quatrefoils, joined by stars. Finally, beyond them crossing and re-crossing, are the seven links of a double festoon.

The large fanlight at No. 69 Merrion Square North LEFT has the same gothick air as those at Gloucester Place, London (page 46) and Rodney Street, Liverpool (page 109), but here there is a lantern and gothick side lights, which now contain leaded lights.

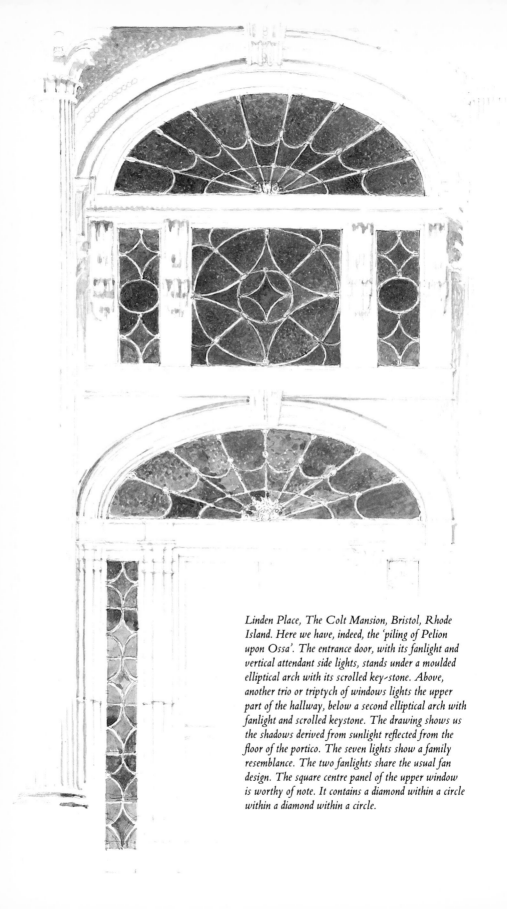

Linden Place, The Colt Mansion, Bristol, Rhode Island. Here we have, indeed, the 'piling of Pelion upon Ossa'. The entrance door, with its fanlight and vertical attendant side lights, stands under a moulded elliptical arch with its scrolled key-stone. Above, another trio or triptych of windows lights the upper part of the hallway, below a second elliptical arch with fanlight and scrolled keystone. The drawing shows us the shadows derived from sunlight reflected from the floor of the portico. The seven lights show a family resemblance. The two fanlights share the usual fan design. The square centre panel of the upper window is worthy of note. It contains a diamond within a circle within a diamond within a circle.

Fanlights of Colonial and Federal America

Tony Birks-Hay

Fanlights in North America followed the same path as those of Britain—from simple wooden designs to iron and leaded versions of greater and greater complexity. A very widespread use of a transom light consisting of a horizontal elongated rectangle divided, for practical reasons, into square panels by vertical bars served across New England to allow light into the hallways of farmhouses from the earliest examples to those of the mid eighteenth century. They were characteristic of the town of Williamsburg, where the first sash windows had been introduced in 1695. From the time of the earliest settlements, house construction was mainly in wood, a material in which arches are not functional, and it is not surprising that the trabeated style was used for the overdoor windows at the same time as brick arches were providing the form for fanlights in London.

Traditional architectural forms, and more particularly plans, were constructed by German, Welsh, Scandinavian and other settlers, and where these houses survive in New England the transplanted national or regional character is very obvious. The architect as a professional did not exist in America much before 1800, and the business of house design and construction was carried out by carpenters. As early as 1724, in Philadelphia, ten of the leading 'master builders' formed themselves into The Carpenters' Company to regulate the building trade and foster higher standards. The standard of craftsmanship was high, but was carried out by a group in society characteristically slow to accept new ideas. When neo-Classicism arrived from Europe in the eighteenth century, therefore, there was a wholesale grafting of a mode of architectural expression, already interpreted in stone in Britain on to the New England clapboard tradition. In matters of detail, design had come full circle with the timber-inspired triglyphs and modillions of stone Greek entablatures reinterpreted in wood on the door surrounds of timber homes.

To the aid of the craftsman came some of the pattern books popular in England. James Gibbs and Colen Campbell, Batty Langley and William Halfpenny all

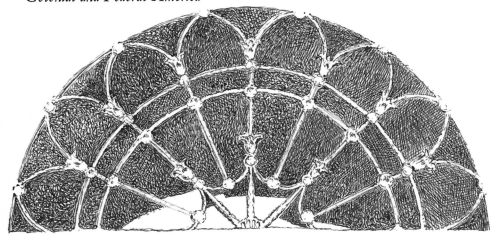

A feature of this classic fanlight from Beacon Hill, Boston, Mass. is that four minor spokes spring from the centre of graduated arches linking the three major spokes, thus creating a corona-like hub.

circulated in due course, but notable was the publication in 1775 (forty years after its appearance in England) by Robin Bell of Swan's *British Architect*, and a little later Pain's *Practical Builder*, under the name *The Practical House Carpenter or Youth's Instructor*.

It is well known that distinguished eighteenth-century Americans such as Jefferson and Judge Hamilton were intimately involved in the design of their own homes. The wealthy heads of families who were in a position to commission the building of substantial houses, were, according to Eberlein and Hubbard (*American Georgian Architecture*) 'frequently, if not generally, their own architects. Some knowledge of architecture was deemed essential to every gentleman's education .... Splendid books of architectural design were in every private library worthy of the name....'

Be that as it may, from the owner's rough sketch it was a craftsman-builder's job to translate this into three-dimensional reality. The resulting doorways, so often the focus of the house, exhibit a high degree of skill in execution, but sometimes a tentative combination of oddly assorted design features. For instance, the Linden House at Danvers, Massachusetts, has a semicircular fanlight built into the top of a very large door—in 1754. A splendid example of an early spoked fanlight of the simplest type, which was to supplant the plain rectangular transom light, is seen in the Golden Ball Tavern at Weston, Massachusetts, dated 1753. An elliptical version, under a severe classical canopy, occurs in Ipswich, Massachusetts, in 1776 at Sally Choate House. These two buildings are both wooden double-fronted houses.

One aspect of the neo-Classical fashion was symmetry, and a great majority of American houses were double-fronted, detached buildings with a central doorway on which most of the decoration was focused. Within a classically inspired doorcase, the semicircular or elliptical fanlight became very popular.

An essential difference between the English and American model relates to the

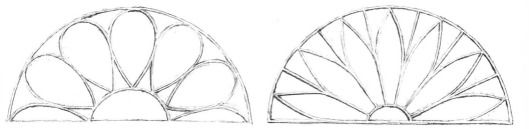

Flower designs at Arlington House, Washington D.C. LEFT *(the entrance to the morning room) and* RIGHT *at Powel Hill, 244 South 3rd Street, Philadelphia, dating from 1768.*

availability of space—or the lack of it. While Edinburgh, Bristol and, of course, London were trying to cram decently spacious houses into narrow sites, and needed fanlights to illuminate long narrow hallways, no such constraints applied in America and there was no need for the door-and-two-window units in a terrace so characteristic of the English Georgian town. In America fanlighted terraces exist, but most of the existing examples from the eighteenth and early nineteenth century are in detached houses.

Centred between sash windows of a 'Palladian' facade, the doorway, often slightly raised above steps, would have pilasters or engaged columns or paired detached columns under a pedimented roof or canopy to create what was called a 'vestibule' before the door. This characteristic roofed projection meant that, to serve its lighting function at all, the fanlight had to be very large, and from about 1775 was often supplemented with side windows on either side of the door to increase the lighting and eventually to provide scope for an all-embracing design motif which wrapped itself all around the door. Sometimes the side lights gave the doorway the appearance of a Palladian or Venetian window (such windows were in any case commonly placed above the door on the first storey), but more often the fanlights would span the side windows as well, and became elliptical for the very practical reason that if semicircular they would demand too much internal height.

These fine side-lighted fanlights, and their cousins in Dublin, in some cases overcame this particular problem by having the outer section of the semicircular fan made of decorated plaster, like Boodle's Club in St James's, London. Probably the most successful fanlights aesthetically are those in which attached columns provide the doorjambs and lie between the side lights under a straight transom, as in Dublin. The confusion to the eye of having detached free-standing columns with a complex fanlight behind did not, however, deter builders from making some of the most intricate designs, or indeed from using similarly complex fanlights as room dividers in the interior of the house.

In Colonial times, cast-iron and lead fanlights were imported from England though this trade dried up in the early Federal period, which coincided with the flowering of fanlight ornament. The credit for applying Adam designs to North America must go to the two most famous names in American architecture of the period—Samuel McIntire, who called himself a 'carver', and Charles Bulfinch, who was as close as one could be at the end of the eighteenth century to being a professional architect. He is described by Fiske Kimball as 'a professional in the nature and extent of his practice, if not his training.'

McIntire's influence was widespread from 1783 onwards. He is most closely associated with Salem, Massachusetts, and his original drawings and papers are in the Essex Institute there. Similarly, Bulfinch is linked with Boston, and it is at Chestnut Street in Salem and Beacon Hill in Boston that the best known terraces of fanlighted houses are to be found, see pages 135, 141–3. It is unfortunate that for want of space most of these fanlights have to be shown without their side lights. Adam designs, festooned fans, batswings, wheels, intercepting circles, lozenges, hearts and diamonds intricately made in lead gain by their juxtaposition, and the shape of the fans ranges from the semicircular to the more severe long rectangles which succeeded them. Many date from the first decade of the nineteenth century.

While Bulfinch and McIntire dominate Boston and Salem, others are associated with the fanlights which grace other American towns down the Eastern seaboard and into the heartland, in particular Ezra Waite (house builder and general carver from London) in Charleston, South Carolina, Gabriel Maingault, who introduced Adam designs to the same city, William Buckland in Maryland and the English-trained John Aviss in Virginia. Fortunately those of their works which have survived (much of Bulfinch's work in Boston is destroyed) are exceptionally well preserved and documented with measured drawings, which include the fanlights, and they are featured in a host of publications on Colonial and Federal period architecture. That they should be both better known and better preserved than their British and Irish counterparts is a tribute to the American interest in conservation, and it is interesting that more than 350 architectural conservation societies exist for the eastern states alone.

The following pages can only hint at the variety and invention of the American fanlight, the shape of which was also used internally and as repeated fenestration on mezzanine floors in the massive city mansions, and even in shop windows. Sometimes the fan would appear within the entablature of a door frame, or repeated up the tower of a church, as at Middlebury, Vermont (page 136), where the upper designs are of the gothick variety, with narrow glazing bars. Salem College, North Carolina, illustrated on page 137, has a charming and fairly common ogee version of this, while an adjoining building has the same design in the round head of a window under the clock.

The smallest fanlight in this book is from America, on page 135, and so is the largest: the apotheosis of the ebullient and exhibitionist architecture of the time must be the triple-decker fanlight of the Colt mansion, 'Linden Place', Bristol, Rhode Island, illustrated on page 130 and built by George de Woolf in 1810.

ABOVE *A tiny fanlight at 'Beverly' on the Pocomoke River, Maryland. As can be seen, the lintel of the door is wider than the brick arch which surrounds the fanlight.*

The wide hallways of many colonial American houses enabled the front door to have side lights. If the overdoor light was the traditional 'fan' light, the side lights were given a pattern distinct from it. If the overdoor light was a long narrow rectangle, a similar pattern could be applied to all three. Such is the doorway at 47 Chestnut Street, Beacon Hill, Boston, ABOVE where ovals and diamonds alternate. At 73 Mount Vernon Street, Beacon Hill, TOP instead of alternating with the ovals and rounds, the diamonds occupy them.

135

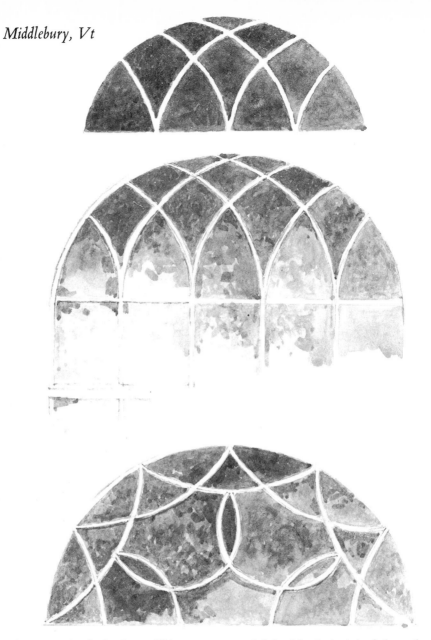

The Congregational Church at Middlebury, Vermont was built by Asher Benjamin in 1806–9, and restored in 1989. Over the west door is the fanlight ABOVE, *where curves of two different radii create an unusual pattern of points and loops. Above it, as part of a Palladian or Venetian window, is the gothick fanlight design* CENTRE *and atop all within the pediment, is the semicircular light* TOP *exactly like the late eighteenth-century gothick fanlights of English country towns.*

Salem, North Carolina, was founded in 1716 by members of the Moravian Church. In 1913 it was annexed to the City of Winston. This beautiful doorway and fanlight RIGHT *are in Salem College, founded in 1772 for Moravian women and girls. The eighteenth-century gothick style of the fanlight under an elliptical arch is the result of interlacing five ogee arches of metal. A similar design is seen higher up, occupying a half-round arch, under the clock of the adjacent building.*

ABOVE *The Hunter House, near Yellow House, Penn. The wooden doorcase, with its conventional fanlight, contrasts with the rubble stone wall in which it is set.*

LEFT *Crosby House, South Brookfield, Mass. Dated 1797, this wooden doorway is set in the clapboard wall of a wooden house. A pair of lovely fluted Corinthian pilasters supports the wooden arch, while the abacus moulding of the capitals is carried across as a transom. The side lights have each eight segments, four form a diamond in the centre, and four more crossing over the centre diamond form a figure eight. A richly moulded keystone between a pair of voussoirs crowns the arch, all of wood.*

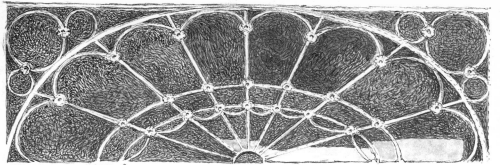

ABOVE *A delicate elliptical fanlight of Adam design within a rectangular frame
at Chestnut Street, Salem, Mass. Compare the side lights with the photograph
opposite, and pages 135 and 146.*

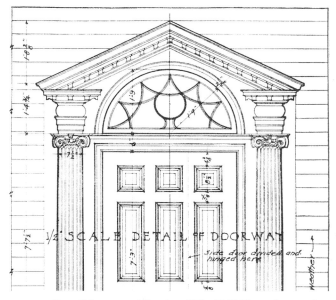

½ SCALE DETAIL OF DOORWAY

side door divided and
hinged here

ABOVE *Part of the measured drawing of The Field House, Longmeadow,
Mass. by Kenneth Clark, shows the classical doorway. In the fanlight
BELOW interlaced segmental curves surround a most unusual figure, echoed
in the Venetian window above it and a fanlight in the pediment.*

LEFT *10 Limehouse Street, Charleston, South Carolina. In a city famous for its historic fanlights, this
substantial doorway contains a deep fanlight, door and narrow side lights under a heavy broken pediment.
The arch in the fanlight is more than a semicircle. The nine spokes do not radiate from its centre, and
are therefore of unequal length. Compare this form with the extended form in the drawing ABOVE TOP.*

141

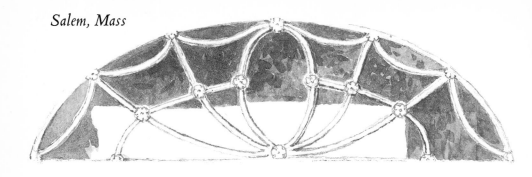

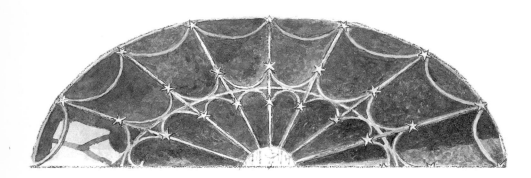

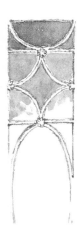

Fanlights and side lights from Chestnut Street, Salem, Mass. The best fanlights of Colonial and early Republican days can be found in houses larger than normal terrace houses, houses where space allowed for a wide entrance hall leading to a graceful 'geometrical' staircase. This wide hall allowed lights to be set at each side of the entrance door which was in two leaves. To fit within the height of the hall, the arch in which the fanlight is set is elliptical or segmental. Of the six examples illustrated here, all from a single street, three (ABOVE) are of the true fan design, and three RIGHT have ingenious arrangements of interlacing circles and diamonds independent of ribs. ABOVE TOP The six spokes spring from a single star, the centre pair combining into an ellipse. All spokes here are curved.

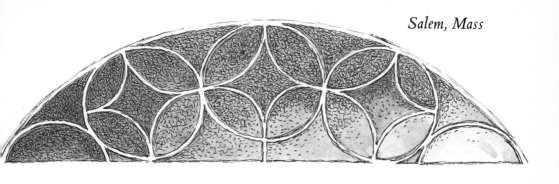

The three designs of circles and diamonds ABOVE *show much ingenuity and resemble the wheels of a watch, especially where their diamond centres are canted, creating the illusion of the escapement wheel in motion. Because of their uncompromising shape the side lights of all six examples, of which only two are illustrated on these pages, bear a resemblance to chain designs of ovals and diamonds.*

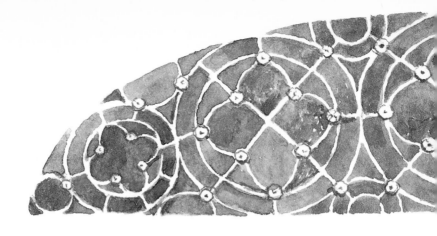

Bibliography

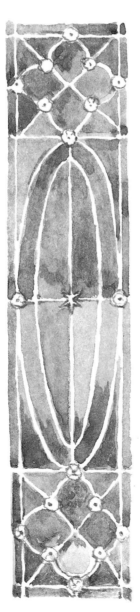

The United States of America

Chamberlain, S. *The New England Image* New York 1962.

Cornelius, C.O. 'Some Early American Doorways', *Bull. of Soc. for the Preservation of New England Antiquities/Bull. of Metropolitan Museum of Art*, Jan. 1928.

Eberlein, H.D., and C. Van Dyke Hubbard *American Georgian Architecture* New York, 1952.

Grossman J., and C. Bruce *Revelations of New England Architecture, People and their Buildings* New York, 1975.

Haas, I. *America's Historic Houses and Restorations* New York, 1966.

The Historic Buildings Survey and The Historic American Engineering Record *Historic America: Buildings, Structures and Sites.* Washington. D.C., 1983.

Kimball, F. *Domestic Architecture of the American Colonies and of the Early Republic* New York, 1927.

————*Mr Samuel McIntire Carver, the Architect of Salem* Portland, Maine, 1940.

Major, H. *The Domestic Architecture of the Early American Republic* Philadelphia, 1926.

McAlister, V., and L. *A Field Guide to American Houses* New York, 1984.

Miller, J.F. *The Architects of the American Colonies* 1968.

Pratt, R., and D. *The First Treasury of Early American Homes* New York, 1949, 1954.

Waterman, T.T., and J.A. Barrows *Domestic Colonial Architecture of Tidewater Virginia* New York, 1968.

Whitehead, F.R., and F.C. Brown (eds) *Survey of Early American Design* New York, republished 1977.

————*Colonial Architecture in New England* New York, republished 1977.

————*Colonial Architecture in Massachusetts* New York, republished 1977.

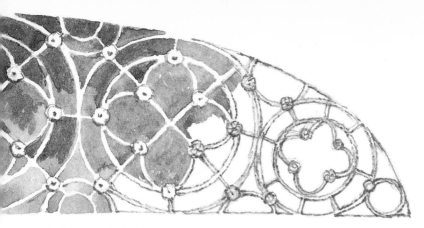

The fanlights and side lights of No. 39 Chestnut Street, Salem, Mass.

Great Britain and Ireland

Bowyer, J. (ed) *A Handbook of Building Crafts* London and New York. A commentary on Peter Nicholson's *The New Practical Builder and Workman's Companion* of 1823.

Colvin, H.M. *A Biographical Dictionary of English Architects 1660–1840* London, 1954, 1978.

Craig, M. *Dublin 1660–1860* Dublin, 1969.

———*The Architecture of Dublin from the Earliest Times to 1880* London, 1982.

———and F. Desmond, the Knight of Glin *Ireland Observed* Cork, 1970.

Cruikshank, D. *A Guide to the Georgian Buildings of Dublin.*

———and P. Wyld *London, The Art of Georgian Building* London and New York, 1975.

Cunliffe, B. *The City of Bath* Gloucester, 1986.

Edinburgh New Town Conservation Committee *The Care and Conservation of Georgian Houses* London, 1986.

Gomme, A., M. Jenner and B. Little *Bristol: An Architectural History* London, 1979.

Guinness, D. *Georgian Dublin* London, 1979.

Harris, J. *English Decorative Ironwork from Contemporary Source Books, 1610–1836* London, 1960.

Ison, W. *The Georgian Buildings of Bath from 1700–1830* Bath, 1948, 1969 and 1980.

———*The Georgian Buildings of Bristol* 1952.

Rasmussen, S.E. *London, the Unique City* London, 1937 and 1960.

Summerson, Sir J. *Heavenly Mansions* London, New York and Markham, Ontario. Containing an essay on 'John Wood and the English Planning Tradition'.

———*Georgian London* London, 1945, 1988.

———*Architecture in Britain 1530–1830* London, Melbourne and Baltimore, 1953.

Survey of London London, *passim*.

Swarbrick, J. *The Lives and Works of Robert and James Adam* London, 1915.

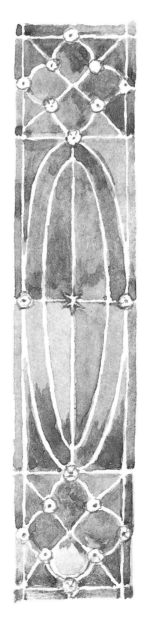

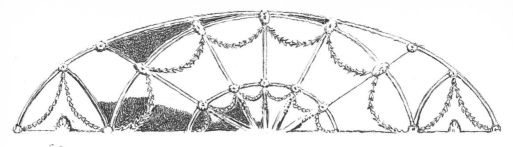
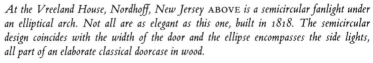

At the Vreeland House, Nordhoff, New Jersey ABOVE *is a semicircular fanlight under an elliptical arch. Not all are as elegant as this one, built in 1818. The semicircular design coincides with the width of the door and the ellipse encompasses the side lights, all part of an elaborate classical doorcase in wood.*

Acknowledgements

The drawing on page 15 is courtesy the British Architectural Library, RIBA, London. The diagrams on pages 21 and 24 are by John Sambrook. All photographs were specially taken by Jane Whitton, except for those on page 9, from *The Practical Exemplar of Architecture*, page 22 by Tony Birks-Hay, pages 18, 23, 25 and 35 by John Sambrook, and pages 123, 127 and 128 by Gordon T. Ledbetter. The photographs on pages 137, 139 and 140 are by courtesy of Mills Lane, The Beehive Press, Savannah, Georgia, USA; on page 138 by courtesy of the Historic American Building Survey. In addition, valuable assistance photographic and otherwise has been provided by Adam Birks-Hay, Gill Black, Mary Clark, Lorna Condon of the Society for the Preservation of New England Antiquities, Edinburgh New Town Conservation Committee, Stephen Harrison, Bay Haseler, Grahame Ledson, Beth Meyer, Jay Patrick and Margaret Thomas.

The side lights at 49 Chestnut Street, Beacon Hill, Boston match those at No. 47 next door (see page 135), but above them is a fascinating design made entirely from interlacing semicircles — superior to Underwood's design in Arundel, on page 99.

Index

This index is for buildings illustrated, by town (with county or state) and street or road, where appropriate.

Arundel, Sussex
  High St, 1
  Maltravers St, 99

Bath, Avon
  Bathwick St, 99
  Cavendish Pl, 92
  Gay St, 97
  George St, 94
  Hay Hill, 98
  Lansdowne Cr, 95
  Portland Pl, 94
  Russel St, 96
  Somerset Pl, 94
Belfast, N. Ireland
  Donegall Pass, 112
Boston, Mass, Beacon Hill, 132
  Chestnut St, 135, 146
  Mt Vernon St, 135
Brighton, East Sussex
  Marine Sq, 103
Bristol, Avon
  Caledonian Pl, Clifton, 104, 105
  Cornwallis Cr, Clifton, 108
  Great George St, 106
  Harley Pl, Clifton, 103, 105, 106
  Royal York Cr, Clifton, 100, 103
  St Michael's Hill, 107
  Sion Hill, Clifton, 104, 105
Bristol, Rhode Island
  Linden Pl, 130
Bury St Edmunds, Suffolk
  Abbey Gate, St, 82
  Chequer Sq, 84
  Guildhall St, 85, 87
  Risby Gate St, 83
  St Anne's Pl, 84
  South Hill Pk, 2
  Westgate St, 84

Castle Cary, Somerset, 87
Charleston, S. Carolina
  Limehouse St, 140
Cheltenham, Glos.

Bath Rd, 91
Clarence Sq, 90
Grafton Rd, 90
Montpellier, 91
Oriel Rd, 91
St George's Ter, 90
Chichester, West Sussex
  Fernleigh Centre, 88
  North St, 88, 89

Dublin, Eire
  Ely Pl, 126
  Fitzwilliam Sq, 124, 125, 129
  Fitzwilliam St, 122
  Hume St, 121, 129
  Leeson St, 124
  Merrion Sq, 123, 126, 127, 128

Edinburgh
  Albany St, 118, 120
  Ann St, 119
  Dundas St, 118, 119
  Great King St, 120
  Hanover St, 117
  India St, 116
  London St, 117
  Melville St, 115, 117
  Moray Pl, 114, 116
  North Castle St, 113
  Northumberland Pl, 120

Farnham, Surrey
  Castle St, 80–2

Liverpool
  Falkner St, 110
  Maryland St, 111
  Rodney St, 109, 111, 112
London
  Abercorn Pl, NW8, 70
  Albemarle St, W1, 40
  Albion St, W2, 66
  Anchor Ter, Southwark, SE1, 76
  Balcombe St, NW1, 49
  Bedford Row, WC1, 18, 38
  Bedford Sq, WC1, 56
  Bryanston Sq, W1, 45
  Camden Rd, NW1, 60

Canonbury Pl, N1, 62
Carlyle Sq, SW3, 75
Catherine Pl, Victoria, SW1, 36
Charlotte St, WC1, 58
Cheyne Wk, SW3, 75
Church Row, Hampstead, NW3, 71–3
Claremont Sq, Islington, N1, 5
Cloudesley Sq, Islington, N1, 63
Cloudesley St, Islington, N1, 60
Colebrook Row, Islington, N1, 61
Connaught Sq, W2, 66
Cunningham Pl, NW8, 70
Devonshire Pl, W1, 51
Dombey St, WC1, 38
Dorset Sq, NW1, 44
Doughty St, WC1, 59
Downing St, SW1, 39
Duke St, W1, 48
Duncan Ter, Islington, N1, 61
Erskine Hill, Hampstead Garden Suburb,
    NW11, 17
Gibson Sq, Islington, N1, 63
Glebe Pl, SW3, 75
Gloucester Pl, S1, 44, 45–7
Grafton St, W1, 55
Granville Sq, WC1, 62
Gt Cumberland Pl, W1, 42
Gt James St, WC1, 37
Gt Ormonde St, WC1, 58
Hamilton Ter, NW8, 67–9
Harley St, W1, 50–1
Harleyford Rd, SE11, 78
Haymarket, SW1, 41
High St, Islington, N1, 32
Hill St, W1, 40
Inglebert St, EC1, 64
Ivor Pl, NW1, 48
Kennington La, SE11, 77
Kennington Rd, SE11, 78
Liverpool Rd, N1, 60
Lloyd St, WC1, 57
Mansfield St, W1, 54–5
Mecklenburgh Sq, WC1, 35
Montagu Sq, W1, 43
Montagu St, W1, 42
Montpelier Row, Blackheath, SE3, 79
Mornington Cr, WC1, 58
Mt Vernon, Hampstead, NW3, 73
Myddleton Sq, Clerkenwell, EC1, 63, 64
The Paragon, Blackheath, SE3, 79

Park Sq, NW1, 49
Portland Pl, W1, 52–3
Portman Sq, W1, 44
Pratt Wk, SE11, 78
Regent Sq, WC1, 57
River St, EC1, 64
St James Sq, SW1, 41
St John St, WC1, 37
St John's Rd, NW8, 69
St Thomas St, Southwark, SE1, 76
Stamford St, SE1, 76
Tavistock Sq, WC1, 57
Trevor Sq, Knightsbridge, SW7, 39
Upper Berkeley St, W1, 41
Upper Cheyne Row, Chelsea, SW3, 74
Upper Wimpole St, W1, 52
Wilkes St, Spitalfields, E1, 65
Wine Office Ct, EC4, 65
Wyndham Pl, W1, 49
York St, Marylebone, NW1, 49

Longmeadow, Mass, 141

Middlebury, Vt
    Congregational Church, 136

Nordhoff, New Jersey, 146

Philadelphia, Penn
    S. 3rd St, 133
Pocomoke R, Maryland, 135

Salem, Mass
    Chestnut St, 141, 142–3, 144–5
Salem, N. Carolina
    Salem College, Winston, 137
South Brookfield, Mass, 138
Stamford, Lincs, 86

Tenterden, Kent
    Ashford Rd, 23
Twickenham, Middlesex
    Marble Hill House, 22

Washington DC, 133
Worcester, Hereford & Worcs
    Bridge St, 25

Yellow House, Penn, 139